GW00494140

COMMUNICATION SKILLS

COMMUNICATION SKILLS

A Practical Handbook

Edited by Chrissie Wright

The Industrial Society

First published in 1993 by
The Industrial Society
Robert Hyde House
48 Bryanston Square
London W1H 7LN
Telephone: 071–262 2401

© The Industrial Society 1993
Reprinted 1994

ISBN 1 85835 018 2

British Library Cataloguing-in-Publication Data.
A catalogue record for this book is available from the
British Library

Typeset by: The Midlands Book Typesetting Company, Loughborough
Printed by: Lavenham Press
Cover design: Integra Communications

Text illustrations (cartoons): Sophie Grillet

ACKNOWLEDGEMENT

The revisions of the material in this book would not have been possible without the kind assistance of Patricia Adams, Anna Amblin, Sonia Arnold, Alan Barker, Mary Overton and Chrissie Wright.

CONTENTS

EFFECTIVE SPEAKING

We spend most of our lives speaking to one another. It is our natural mode of communication.

However, something strange happens to most people when asked to do that same activity in front of a group. A whole host of irrational fears raise their ugly heads. It is an activity many of us would get out of if we could.

Increasingly we are called on at work to make presentations to groups, both large and small, in a variety of situations. We are very often judged by our performance on these occasions. How well do we get over our point of view to those to whom we are speaking?

This book is about speaking effectively. The guidelines can be applied in a variety of speaking situations: making presentations, expressing views at meetings, explaining facts in interviews, briefing the team.

The guide concentrates on three main areas:

- preparation

- how to put the message over effectively

- dealing with nerves.

It will help anyone who is involved in speaking activities to make the experience a successful and, hopefully, enjoyable one.

PREPARATION

There is a saying that goes 'to fail to prepare is to prepare to fail'. This is probably more true of speaking to groups than any other activity you may become involved in at work.

But what do you need to prepare and how do you do it? Rudyard Kipling's famous quote may provide a clue:

'I keep six honest serving-men
(they taught me all I knew)
Their names are What and Why and When
and How and Where and Who.'

By working through the six honest serving-men you can cover all aspects of thorough preparation.

Why, Who, Where and When are looked at in this section. What is dealt with on page 13 and How on page 22.

WHY: DECIDING THE OBJECTIVE

The very first thing to get clear in your mind is the objective of the speech. There will be a general objective as well as a specific objective relating to the subject matter.

General objectives will fall into one of the following categories:

- to persuade or sell

- to teach

- to stimulate thought

- to inform

- to entertain

Whatever your general objective is you always need to try and entertain your audience. This does not mean cracking poor jokes every other sentence. It does, however, mean that the material must be put over in such a way that it is interesting and people want to listen.

The specific objective will depend on the subject matter entirely.

It is an excellent idea to write down the objective of the speech in one sentence. This has various benefits:

- it clears the speaker's mind right at the start

- selection of material can be based on fulfilling the objective

- when your notes are complete you can again check that you are meeting your original aim.

EXAMPLES OF OBJECTIVES:

To persuade Jones and Co to buy our wheel bearings.
To inform the Accounts Department of a new system
designed to keep a closer watch on bad debts.
To stimulate the Women's Institute to think about the
importance of industry.

WHO: RESEARCHING THE AUDIENCE

Anyone who has sat through a speech and wondered if
they are in the right room will know the importance of
this question.

The audience or group you are talking to are the most
important people in the whole exercise. What should you
know about them?

- How many of them are there?

- Why are they there? Are they there of their own
  free will? Were they sent to listen? Are they
  paying?

- What is their present knowledge of the subject of
  the talk?

- Are they likely to have any bias towards or against
  the subject or speaker?

- What are their expectations of the talk and speaker?

- What age range and sex are they?

All the above points will determine the material used
and the approach to the speech. For example, there is a
world of difference between a woman talking to a group
of men about women's equality and a woman talking

to women on the same subject. Similarly a computer expert talking to other computer experts about the latest technology will be able to use far more technical language than would be possible when talking to a group of non-experts.

You have a duty to those who listen to you to make sure your speech is pitched at the right level for them.

Remember you are there to meet the needs of your audience. Good rapport with that audience is the key to success.

WHERE: PREPARING THE ENVIRONMENT

It is important to consider where the talk is going to take place. There may not always be a choice of venue but it is vital to make every effort to see it, especially if you have not spoken there before.

The following points need consideration:

PRACTISING

One's voice can sound disembodied in large echoing rooms. It is better to have tried your voice out beforehand than to be put off by it when you start to speak with the audience present. Practising with the microphone is also important if you have to use one.

If the room is large it is vital to try out the volume of the voice. Plant someone at the back of the room and practise to see if they can hear you.

HOW THINGS IN THE ROOM WORK

On a very practical level, it is useful to know where the light switches are and how the blinds draw if you are using slides or films. Find out how the windows open and close or how the air conditioning works so that you can regulate the temperature if necessary.

DISTRACTIONS

Become aware of any likely distractions for you and your audience.

A speaker who can see interesting things happening outside the window is likely to find it harder to concentrate on the audience. Similarly, if you are speaking in front of a large picture window at Heathrow Airport, your audience is likely to become very interested in jumbo jets taking off and landing and stop listening to what you have to say.

Other distractions like noise and general interruptions need to be catered for where possible.

Unfortunately we do not live in a perfectly ordered world but minimising distractions as far as possible is vital.

SEATING

Seating layouts can vary enormously and again there may be no control over the layout. The following are a few of the many variations possible — there are advantages and disadvantages to each:

THEATRE STYLE

People sit in rows. Most common with large audiences. Formal atmosphere and eye contact with the audience more difficult to achieve.

HORSESHOE

Single row of people arranged in a horseshoe shape. Informal and conducive to participation.

CURVED ROWS

Similar problems as with theatre style but slightly less formal.

CABARET

People sitting in groups around tables. Useful if you want to break the audience into formal discussion groups.

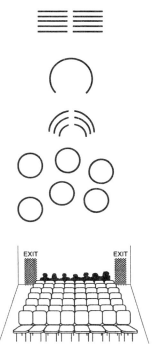

POINTS TO WATCH:

- People have a great tendency to sit at the back of rooms if given the choice. If there are more chairs than audience you may find them all sitting in the back rows. If you anticipate too many chairs, rope off the back rows or have someone directing people to the front as they arrive. Ideally you want the audience as near as possible.

• Try to make sure the seats are not too comfortable. Low, soft chairs can be sleep inducing — the last thing you want from the audience.

The environment you have to speak in can either hinder or help. The aim is to minimise the hindrances and maximise the good points.

WHEN: TIMING

How many times have you heard speakers drone on long after the expected finishing time? They seemingly do not realise the audience is getting restless. Considering the time of day and how long you have for your talk is important.

TIME OF DAY

Time of day can affect the audience. After lunch is known as the graveyard session in training circles. Audiences who have had a few drinks and a good lunch will probably be feeling like an afternoon nap rather than listening to a speech.

The audience may have already sat through several other speakers. How can you make sure they are interested and listen to what you have to say?

HOW LONG HAVE WE GOT — KEEPING TO TIME

Knowing how long you have got and sticking to it is crucial to good talks. This means practising to see whether you have the right amount of material. Most people find that if they practise in their head or to the bathroom mirror the actual speech will take about 25 per cent longer. Using a flip chart or other visual aids will also add considerably to the time. Bear that in mind. If there is no clock in the room, take your watch off and put it on a table near you so that you can glance at it occasionally to check your timing.

CONCENTRATION PROBLEMS

People's ability to concentrate hard for long periods is not too good. You need to anticipate lack of concentration in the audience.

Concentration levels over a two-hour period look something like this:

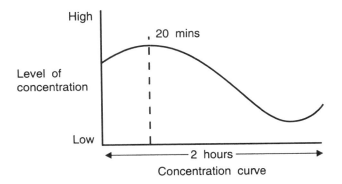

Concentration curve

When listening to a talk concentration is usually fairly good for the first 20 or so minutes. For some people, however, it can be as short as five minutes. Thereafter, maintaining concentration gets harder and harder until they hear the magic words 'in conclusion'. Concentration improves slightly at that point in anticipation of the end of the speech.

This means that you need to find ways of maintaining the audience's interest in what you have to say. This is further discussed on page 23.

OUR OWN BEST TIME

Individually you may have good and less good times of the day. Some people are better first thing in the morning; others late in the afternoon. If you find speaking to a group a nerve-racking experience, it can be wise to try and find a time of day when you feel physically and mentally able to cope with the task. Again this is not always possible, but sometimes can be arranged.

CHECKLIST 1

General preparation

- Why am I speaking?   Clarify objectives
- Who am I speaking to? Research the audience
- Where am I speaking?   Familiarise yourself with the venue and equipment
  Practise your voice
  Anticipate distractions
  Arrange the seating suitably
- When am I speaking?   Time of day
  How long have I got?
  Anticipate lack of concentration

PREPARING THE MATERIAL

Any speech will almost certainly fail unless careful thought is given to the subject matter. Unstructured, rambling talks tend to be difficult to concentrate upon. Unless the main points are made very clear for the audience, the message will be forgotten quickly. The following stages of activity will help you through the preparation of the material and ensure that your speech is well structured and lively.

STAGE ONE: BRAINSTORMING

It is essential to get all thoughts and ideas on your subject down on paper. A useful method for doing this is by making pattern notes. This is a highly creative method of personal brainstorming. For centuries people have organised information in lists in the belief that the brain naturally arranged material in linear form. However, research has shown that the brain is constantly analysing, interpreting and juggling whole interrelated networks of thoughts and ideas. Pattern notes enable the brain to relate to information far more naturally and efficiently, by forming an interrelated pattern rather than a list.

Pattern notes are easy to do.

- Take a plain sheet of paper. Write the objective of your talk at the top, and the main theme of your talk in the centre of the page in a circle.

- Write down all the ideas and thoughts you have on the subject, starting from the circle and branching out along lines of connecting ideas.

- Let your mind be as free as possible. Do not restrict your thoughts by deciding where each point should go in a list. Your ideas should flow easily.

●When finished, circle any related ideas and sections and establish your order of priorities and organisation.

An example of a completed pattern note is given below.

Objective:
To inform a group of prospective home owners about what to consider

Once you have recorded all your immediate ideas, it is a good idea to put them to one side for a while. When you return to the notes, you may have thought of other ideas to add. Group common themes or ideas together. If the logical ordering of points was not obvious at first, after a break, invariably, you can see how it all fits together.

STAGE TWO: STRUCTURING AND SELECTING

Most people at this stage have a mass of possible ideas and information they could use — usually far too much material for the time they have for the speech.

It is important to keep the number of main points to a minimum. In a 45-minute speech you should not try to make more than seven main points. Certainly in a five-minute speech it is difficult to do justice to more than one or two main points. This may not seem very many, but if you are to leave the audience with a very clear picture of what you have said you cannot expect them to remember masses and masses of points.

You should concentrate on and write the middle of the speech first. Opening and closing is discussed in Stage four.

Selecting the material you are going to use should be dictated by the following:

- The objective — is some of the information you have irrelevant to the objective of the speech?

- The audience — do they know most of this already?

- How long have I got?

●MUST, SHOULD, COULD — sometimes it is possible to select on the basis of what the audience must, should and could know. For example, when talking to a group about the organisation's new appraisal system, we *must* tell them how it will operate and their involvement in the system. We *should* tell them why the decision has been made to install the system. We *could* tell them why this particular system has been chosen against any other.

This stage is often the hardest. It is always tempting to tell people everything you know about a subject especially if it is one you know well. The more you know, the more disciplined and discriminating you need to be. Be highly selective to suit your audience.

The structure of a talk should follow the pattern of:

●Tell 'em what you're going to tell 'em.

●Tell 'em.

●Tell 'em what you've told 'em.

Like news bulletins on the television, you need to tell people what you are going to cover in your speech, then expand on each of those points, and finish by summarising what you have said, reiterating the main points again.

The following structure is useful to adopt when presenting a case or trying to persuade people of your view:

●State the proposition.

●Anticipate objections — concede any flaws in the argument. Even if you do not express them out loud, it is important to consider what they might be and select your material appropriately.

- Prove your case — select your best reasons for your proposition. Do not overload your talk with lots of reasons. Quality is better than quantity.

- Show your practical evidence — build in practical examples of the facts you are relying upon. Do not slant the evidence.

- End by repeating the proposition.

It makes for much easier listening if you alert your audience to the structure you are using. This is akin to using headings and paragraphs when writing.

Therefore when you actually deliver your speech it is important to state the *linkages* — *'so let's look now at the second area I want to cover'*.

Another device which works well is using rhetorical questions i.e. *'Why should we consider this subject?'* or *'Which do we need to think about in implementing this plan?'* Again this provides sign posts to the audience and will generally make your speech easier to follow.

STAGE THREE: ILLUSTRATING

Whenever you speak to a group of people you are competing with their own vivid imaginations. When you are listening to people talk, you can easily find yourself drifting off into your own little world.

Most people have mental images or pictures in their minds. As a speaker you need to talk in pictures and give them to the audience rather than let them drift off into their own.

This often means simplifying confusing figures into something concrete and real.

Illustrating what you are saying with real life examples is important too.

EXAMPLE:

An accountant talking to a group about the basic principles of auditing could illustrate his talk with the problems of stocktaking a Welsh hill farm with the sheep scattered over the hills.

Finding the examples is crucial where the subject matter is basically boring. You do not always have exciting subjects to speak about. However, careful thought can usually yield suitable illustrations from your own experiences.

STAGE FOUR: OPENING AND CLOSING A TALK

Only when you have completely sorted out the main part of your speech should you think about opening and closing since the content of the middle will dictate these.

INTRODUCTION

The introduction can be looked at like this:

I   Interest
N   Need
T   Title
R   Ratings
O   Objective

INTEREST

Find something to capture the attention of the audience immediately. Preferably not the usual lines like *'unaccustomed as I am to public speaking'*.

NEED

Show the audience why they need to listen to what you have got to say. What is the relevance to them?

TITLE AND RATINGS

This is the 'Tell 'em what you're going to tell 'em' part. Tell them the subject of your talk and what you are going to cover.

OBJECTIVE

You may or may not decide to state this explicitly. If you do not, the objective should shine through to your audience.

CLOSING

The closing section of your talk should be just that. It should be conclusive. It should not just drift to a halt with words like 'I think that's all I've got to say'. Remember that what you say last is the last thought you leave with your audience. Therefore, if you want to stimulate them into some action, you should tell them what to do next. You should summarise your main points again as part of the 'Tell 'em what you've told 'em' routine.

It is essential to write out your opening and closing sentences in full and incorporate them into your notes (see Stage Five). The opening sentence will help to get you started and when you have uttered the closing line you will know you have come to the end, hence avoiding drifting to a halt.

STAGE FIVE: NOTES

Notes should be brief and consist of key words. Speakers who use verbatim notes are really reading out aloud rather than speaking from within. Also completely written out speeches sound stilted even if learned by heart. This is because written English and spoken English are not the same.

If you are making a particularly important speech, it is an excellent idea to write the whole thing out in full,

practise, and then reduce it all to key notes. Not only will
you then be speaking rather than reading, but you will
be able to look at the audience rather than having to keep
your eyes on the page so as not to lose your place.

Notes are best put on cards. There are various good
reasons for this:

- they do not shake around as
  much as sheets of paper if
  you are nervous

- you do not need a lectern
  to prop up all the sheaves of
  paper, as cards can be held
  quite easily

- since they are smaller, they
  encourage you to use key
  words rather than writing
  down complete sentences.

Some of the basic rules that follow will help to ensure
that what you do put on cards will be useful.

KEY WORDS

It is essential to use the right words otherwise you may
look at the card and wonder what on earth it was you
meant by *environment*, for example.

USE YOUR OWN HANDWRITING

Make your notes in your own handwriting written
large. Typewritten notes are invariably too small to see
comfortably. This may mean that you only have two
or three key words on a card. It is much better to have
several cards than one with everything crammed on.

WRITE TIMINGS ON THE CARDS

As a good check of how fast or slow you are going, it can be useful to write a note to yourself at the point when you expect to be halfway through, for example. If you are only halfway through a 30 minute talk at the 20-minute stage, you will need to speed up or cut out some of the material.

WRITE MESSAGES TO YOURSELF WITH DIFFERENT COLOURED PENS

For example, if you talk too fast write SLOW DOWN in your notes. If you are not too good at looking at the audience write LOOK UP/ROUND ROOM and so on. When you are up there talking you are probably concentrating 100 per cent on what you are saying. These sorts of notes can remind you occasionally of other points to remember.

CLIP THE CARDS TOGETHER

If you have more than one card do clip them together. Treasury tags are useful for this purpose. Whatever you do, number the cards so that even if they become separated you can get them back together in the proper order quickly.

Finally, practise with cards, especially if you have not used them before.

CHECKLIST 2

Preparing the material

- Brainstorm the subject
  Make pattern notes

- Structure and select
  Keep the number of main points down to an appropriate level

  Select on the basis of — objective, time, audience, must, should, could
  Tell it like the news —
    tell 'em what you're going to tell 'em
    tell 'em
    tell 'em what you've told 'em

- Use illustrations
    Simplify difficult or complex information
    Use real-life examples to illustrate points

- Opening and closing
    Write opening and closing sentences in full
    Be challenging and capture the audience in the opening
    Be conclusive when you finish

- Notes
    Notes on cards
    Use key words
    Write timings and messages to yourself on cards
    Clip them together

- Practise timing

PUTTING YOURSELF ACROSS

Having done all this work in preparing your talk, it should in theory be easy to get up and deliver it. Not so! While the subject of nerves is dealt with on page 000, there are various important aspects to consider relating to how you put your message across.

Although our basic communication medium is words, it is surprising how little contribution to the message they have on their own. Some research by Albert Mehrabian reveals the following information about the percentage contribution to the total message:

> 7% verbal — to do with words
> 38% vocal — to do with tone of voice
> 55% visual — to do with facial expression, gesture, posture and so on.

Let us take each of these areas in turn:

WORDS

The words used will be determined by the audience. Only use jargon in its rightful place. Be aware of the problems involved with words.

EXAMPLE:

Talking about pikelets to a group from the Midlands would be acceptable. To a group from London it would not. (For those of you who do not know what they are, they are crumpets or muffins.)

Use concrete, simple language. Do not talk in abstractions. Do not use five words when one would do, e.g. "in the fullness of time" — i.e. "soon" or "now" would be better. Be conscious of using positive words. Avoid words like "but", "try", "maybe" etc. Avoid sexist and racist language. The ladder of abstraction given below shows the different levels of abstraction which could be used to describe Betsy, the cow.

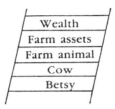

Keep towards the lower levels of the ladder. Talk in sentences. Just as you would write in sentences you should try to talk in them too. A talk which is strung together with ands and buts can be very difficult to follow.

HOW WE SAY IT

The quite large contribution that this makes to your message is important to consider. Sarcasm, for example, relies almost totally on the way you say the words. *'You're coming home with me tonight'* could be said in a variety of ways, with very different meanings!

You contribute to the understanding of the message in a variety of ways:

EXPRESSION

The amount of emphasis placed on particular words will focus attention on important points. You can show how enthusiastic you are by injecting expression into what you are saying. If you are not enthusiastic about your subject, you can hardly expect your audience to be.

PAUSING

Do not be afraid of pausing. You do not have to rush through it all like an express train. Give the audience time to take in and digest what you are saying. Certainly, pause after the main points of your talk.

HAM IT UP

You need to use more expression than usual when talking to a large group. You need to ham it up quite considerably to have the same effect as you would have with a group of, say, five. Do not be afraid of this. You have to go quite a long way before you are in danger of going over the top.

TONE OF VOICE AND PITCH

There is nothing more tedious than listening to a speech delivered in a monotonous tone of voice. A voice that moves up and down like a piano scale is much more interesting. Try practising and listening to your voice with a tape recorder.

SPEAK CLEARLY

Try to make sure that words do not run into one another. If there are tongue twisting words in your talk, practise them so that they come out perfectly. The exercises on page 43 can help with articulation generally. Be conscious of "bringing your voice forward in your mouth". Do open your mouth when you speak.

SPEAK OUT NOT UP

Most people give up on a speaker they have to strain to hear. Make sure you are loud enough for everyone in the room. Breathing properly can help here. Lungs are rather like an organ. If you do not put enough air into them you get a rather squeaky sound out. Practise breathing deeply. This can help quell nerves as well, but do not overdo it or you may pass out!

BODY LANGUAGE

A quite outstanding contribution to your message is made by all those things you do not actually say: the way you stand, the gestures you use, whether you look miserable or happy. Unfortunately, in the unnatural environment of speaking to a group, nervous mannerisms can take over: you cannot bear to look at the audience so you stare at your notes or some point above their heads, you shuffle around or pace up and down. How can you overcome these problems?

LOOK AT THE AUDIENCE

This may be very hard to do but is essential. You need to look at them to see how they are reacting. Are they bored? Asleep? Looking interested? Looking at you? You want to worry when the audience stops looking at you for any length of time. It is usually indicative of not listening. In small groups you should look at everyone and at eye level, not above their heads. If people are arranged in a horseshoe shape, you must make sure you look at the people on the extreme right and left and not just those towards the back. In a large group the easiest way to maintain eye contact is to draw a large M or W round the room. This will encompass everyone.

Eye contact is vital in order to maintain audience interest in what you have to say.

SMILE

Again quite hard to do if you are nervous. Even if you are not particularly happy, smiling can create the illusion that you are. It is also surprising how very often the audience smile back. Smiling also has the added benefit of relaxing your vocal chords — it can help to make your voice sound more interesting.

AVOID CREATING BARRIERS

You need to get as near to your audience as possible. Standing behind a desk or lectern immediately sets up a barrier. It is always tempting to hide behind something, but is undesirable.

STAND SQUARE

Find a comfortable stance. The best position is standing with feet slightly apart. Try to avoid leaning up against furniture, and keep hands out of pockets.

BEWARE OF DISTRACTING MANNERISMS

This does not mean standing rigid. Most of us use our hands to some extent to add emphasis to what we are

saying and we should not stop doing this. However, waving your arms around all over the place is likely to distract the audience. Jangling keys and coins in pockets or wearing clanking jewellery can also distract. The major problem with distracting mannerisms is that if the audience hooks on to them, it will concentrate on them rather than listening to your message.

BE NATURAL

Easier said than done, you may say. However, if you concentrate on getting the message across and stop

worrying about yourself, you will have more chance of coming over naturally.

The best way of making sure you have got most of these points right is to practise. The most effective way is in front of a video camera so that you can see yourself as others see you. This is not possible for many. Alternatively try practising in front of the family or a group of friends and asking them to criticise honestly. Without constructive feedback on how you come over you cannot hope to iron out any problems, or improve.

CHECKLIST 3

Making sure you are understood

Words	Use simple words
	Avoid jargon
	Talk in concrete rather than abstract language
How we say it	Use expressions in voice
	Build in pauses
	Ham it up
	Develop a range of tone and pitch in voice
	Speak clearly
	Speak out
What we do not say	Look at the audience
	Smile
	Avoid creating physical barriers
	Stand square
	Beware of distracting mannerisms
	Be natural

DIFFERENT METHODS OF PUTTING THE MESSAGE OVER

There are many ways open to you to vary the way you actually approach your subject. In longer talks finding some way of involving the audience can be helpful in overcoming the concentration problem.

The following alternatives may be useful to consider:

AUDIENCE PARTICIPATION

You might be able to split the audience into groups, ask them to discuss a particular topic and then report back to the whole group. This is particularly useful in a training situation.

QUESTION AND ANSWER SESSIONS

It is almost always desirable to invite questions from the audience, but in a structured way. Question sessions are usually best left until the end of the talk, but if the session is a long one, breaking up the talk with short question sessions may be useful. How to set up a question session is discussed in the next section.

LECTURING

If you are going to talk to your audience for any length of time without participation from them, you must break up the talk in other ways, possibly by using visual aids of some sort (see page 32).

You need to find the best approach bearing in mind the time available and the objective. When the audience participates it can all take much longer. Keep that in mind.

DEALING WITH QUESTIONS

There are good reasons for inviting questions from the audience. The main one is that it helps to contribute towards the message being understood. If one person asks a question about some aspect they are not clear on, it will help everyone else in the audience.

It is important to tell people there will be an opportunity to ask questions at the end of the talk. As they listen questions may occur to them and they can save them up. This is better than springing the idea on the audience at the end.

Sometimes you may have a chairperson to deal with questions and this can help. The chairperson will ask for questions from the audience, watch the time, repeat the question so the audience can all hear it, and if a panel of speakers is involved indicate who should answer.

If you do not have a chairperson, the following points should be borne in mind:

- Do not expect questions to come immediately after you stop talking. You are asking the audience to take on a different role. They have been listening up until now and may need a few moments to think of the questions they want to ask.

- Have a plant in the audience if necessary. That is, have someone primed to ask a question if they are not forthcoming immediately from the rest of the audience.

- When someone in the audience asks a question, repeat it, so that everyone in the room knows what is being answered.

- Answer as concisely as you can. Do not go on and on, but do not make it so short that it does not answer the question.

- If you do not know the answer, say so. Never on any account invent an answer. Ask the audience if anyone knows the answer or offer to find out.

- Take questions from all over the room. Do not concentrate on a particular group or person if other people want to ask questions.

31

- When time is going fast say *'Just two more questions, please'*.

- If a question is not clear, rephrase it, e.g.: *'Do I understand you to be asking . . .?'*

- If a member of the audience is making a statement rather than asking a question, say: *'There is a great deal in what you say. May we have the next question please?'*

- If a questioner is hostile, it can be quite useful to ask them to answer the question themselves, e.g.: *'What about X?'* The answer could be: *'Well, maybe you'd like to tell us what you think?'* Whatever you do, try to remain calm and composed.

By following these simple guidelines, question sessions will be productive and will help considerably in creating understanding of the subject in the audience.

VISUAL AIDS

There are many different types of visual aids you can use to complement your talk. It is important to consider using them because:

- They break the whole thing up, which is extremely useful in longer talks.

- They are visual — a different activity for the audience from passive listening.

- They can help illustrate complex information in a simplified way.

What types of visual aids are there?

SLIDES

Either for an overhead projector or a slide projector. Limit the number you use.

FLIP CHART

A board and easel with sheets of paper which can be written on during a talk or prepared beforehand and referred to during a talk.

MODELS

If you are talking about a piece of equipment, it is a good idea to have a model of it there so that people can see and examine it.

FILMS AND VIDEOS

In a training environment, films and videos can often illustrate particular points very usefully.

Be adventurous with visual aids but do not overdo it. The following points give some guidelines on their use:

PLAN

Plan the use of visual aids to complement your talk. However, never rely on them completely. Always be prepared for the worst. If the equipment breaks down you must be able to talk without the visual aids.

KEEP THEM SIMPLE

If using slides, it is essential to simplify the information you are presenting. Columns of figures will not add anything at all, but if the information is turned into a simple graph or bar chart, the visual impact will be much more effective. Do not use too many words on slides. They should not be 'verbal printouts'.

GIVE TIME

Give time for the audience to look at slides. Do not talk and show slides at the same time. When you have moved on from the topic illustrated by the slide take it off. Do not leave the audience looking at something that does not relate to what you are saying.

LIMIT THE NUMBER

Limit the number of visual aids to be used. Do not use them for the sake of it and do not use too many different types. For example, stick to a flip chart and overhead projector, or just use a slide projector. Do not feel compelled to use every aid available in the same presentation.

TALK TO THE GROUP

Do not talk to the screen, flip chart or slide. Stay facing the audience. Do not point to the screen with your arms. If you want to highlight particular points, use a pointer with a slide projector. With an overhead projector use a pencil or pointer on the projector itself, not the screen.

MAKE THEM LARGE AND PUNCHY

Keep slides simple and punchy. If using a flipchart, write in large letters using a black pen. Blue, red and green are quite difficult to see at a distance. Make sure everyone in the room is going to be able to see your visual aids.

CHECK ANY EQUIPMENT

Check any equipment before you start your talk. Practise so that you are familiar with how the equipment works. Check the blinds and lights in the room if you need to darken it. Always be prepared for the worst and have extra bulbs and extension leads available.

Using visual aids can be enormously useful in helping to put over what cannot be said by words alone. Do beware — if slides are poorly produced they will have exactly the opposite effect and will confuse the audience.

Be prepared to cope without them; if there is a power-cut, for example!

CHECKLIST 4

Different methods of putting the message over

Dealing with questions	Give time for audience to think
	Repeat the question
	Answer concisely
	Never make up an answer
	Take questions from all parts of the audience
	Deal with difficult questions calmly
Visual aids	Plan them
	Keep them simple
	Give audience time to take in
	Limit the number
	Talk to the group
	Make them large and punchy
	Check equipment

DEALING WITH NERVES

A common reaction to being asked to speak to a group is one of sheer terror. It is one of the top ten human fears, along with spiders and heights. It is worth taking comfort from the fact. You are not alone.

Do not be fooled, however, into thinking that nerves disappear once you have become used to speaking to groups. They do not.

There is an old saying that says that the day you have no nerves is the day to stop. There is a good physiological reason for this. When you are nervous your adrenalin flows. Adrenalin is what tones you up to deal with problem situations. What you have to do is use that adrenalin to help.

The other important fact of life is that however nervous and shaky you may feel inside, the audience hardly ever notices. People will only notice if you start behaving unnaturally. Unfortunately, some nervous mannerisms do get recognised by audiences. You can see shaking hands, for example. You can also see worried expressions.

To a certain extent you all have to find your own way of controlling your nerves.

The following suggestions may be useful, however, as they have certainly worked for other people.

PREPARE THOROUGHLY

If you have done all you possibly can in preparing your material and researching the audience, it provides a degree of security. Preparing speeches takes time, so make sure you allow enough.

BEWARE OF THE SELF-FULFILLING PROPHECY

If you think the audience will react in a hostile way, it is easy to become defensive. Defensiveness is one of those characteristics that can easily come over in tone of voice and body language. The audience will then react on that basis and may well become hostile. This is a trap which many fall into. However, if you think the audience is going to like what you have to say, they probably will because you will transmit the right vibrations.

STAND WHERE YOU ARE GOING TO SPEAK

In advance, try to get used to what it feels like standing in the spot you will be speaking from. For example, if you are sitting in a meeting as part of the group and then come to the front to give a short presentation, the room will look completely different. This can be offputting.

TRY OUT YOUR VOICE

This has already been mentioned, but it is important so that you do not experience that disembodied feeling when you start.

DISTRACT YOURSELF FOR TEN MINUTES BEFORE YOU BEGIN

For many people it is those last few moments before you start that are the worst. Try distracting yourself and clear your mind of what is to come. Talk to someone about an unrelated subject or go to the cloakroom. Breathing deeply or doing a few neck exercises can also help.

DRINK

No, this is not to encourage you to blot it all out with alcohol! Some people would say that you should never have a drink before giving a talk. Depending on your capacity ONE drink may help. Whatever you do, do not overdo it. Alcohol gives a false sense of security, as many speakers have discovered to their cost.

NECK EXERCISES

A lot of tension can build up in your neck and shoulders when you are worried or nervous. Try neck rolling. Lean your head right back and gently and slowly roll it right round in a circle so your chin falls forward on your chest. Bring your head back to the start position, rolling it upwards the other way.

BREATHE DEEPLY

As we have already seen this can help voice production. Breathing deeply a couple of times does have a calming effect and can help to control the adrenalin flow.

PREPARE ANSWERS TO ANTICIPATED QUESTIONS

Again, by thinking ahead of what might be asked, you can prepare your answers. This helps that feeling of security.

DO NOT WORRY ABOUT YOURSELF

The important thing about talking to a group is getting the message over. Worry about the subject by all means, but concentrate on that and not yourself.

THE AUDIENCE ARE PROBABLY QUITE NICE PEOPLE REALLY

They are not usually out for blood. It may feel like that but most people do not want to see you fail.

It is quite possible to exude an air of confidence even if you do not feel it. Most important of all is knowing your subject as well as possible. You can gain confidence in your knowledge.

As a final thought on the subject of nerves, think of the very worst thing that could happen to you. Lay your worst horror on the line and think it through. What will you do if you dry up completely? What will the consequences be? How will you cope if it happens? It may not after all be as bad as you think.

THE MECHANICS OF SPEAKING

Most people would rather be ineffective in their speech than run the risk of people's thinking that their speech is exaggerated. We tend to think we are exaggerating when we move even a minute amount away from our 'normal speech' and 'normal speech' is in most cases not at all clear. It is worth bearing in mind that it takes a great effort to make a small change apparent to other people.

Like golf, speech can only be improved by regular practice. A few minutes' practice period each day can work wonders in making your speech more effective.

ARTICULATION

- Practise exaggerated enunciation in front of a glass. People unconsciously lip-read when they are listening and clearly formed words make understanding easier.

- Bite into the consonants and pay special attention to the sounds of P, B, T, D, K and G when they come at the end of a word.

- Vowel sounds are the 'carrier-waves'. Let the sound come out by opening the mouth and see that the sounds are properly formed.

- Develop the resonance in the voice by practising sentences which contain a large number of Ms, Ns and NGs.

A resonant voice:

- carries further
- sounds better

- does not tire or become strained so easily.

- An organ will not play properly unless the supply
  of air is strong and controlled. In the same way
  proper breathing greatly helps the sound and the
  control of the human voice. The practice of deep,
  regular breathing not only helps the voice but is an
  admirable method of keeping relaxed.

MAKING SPEECH EFFECTIVE

We hold our listeners' attention more through their
feelings than their reason. We convey our intellectual
meaning by the words we use and by their arrangement.
We convey our feelings, that is, our emotional meaning,
by the way in which we speak. To make our words
effective we need to give our attention to tune, tempo,
emphasis and phrasing.

- *Tone*   Most speakers of the English language tend
  to use only two or three tones of the musical scale.
  The Welsh and West Highlanders of Scotland, on
  the other hand, use at least an octave and a half.
  Speech is more meaningful when we use plenty of
  range of tone. Practise increasing the range of tone
  in your voice.

- *Tempo*   Speed of speech is measured by the
  number of spoken words per minute. Pace is
  measured by how quickly the listeners feel the
  time is passing. Speech is more interesting to the
  listeners when the speed is varied. If your average
  speed is too slow your listeners become bored and
  impatient. On the other hand if your average speed
  is too fast your listeners do not have enough time
  to take in what you are saying and once again they
  lose interest.

- *Emphasis*   We put meaning into words by placing emphasis at appropriate points. Emphasise important words and phrases.

- *Phrasing*   The unit of writing is the single word. The unit of speech is the phrase. It is in the moments of silence between phrases, however small, that the listener interprets the meaning. Therefore see that the phrases are separated by pauses so that the listeners can 'get the picture'.

- Do not worry about speaking up – speak out.

- Try not to think of the mechanics of speech while actually talking to people. Train yourself to speak more clearly in a definite practice period and so gradually make the 'artificial' way become the 'natural' way.

- Learn a few passages by heart to practise in spare moments when alone.

EXERCISES IN ENUNCIATION

- 'Red leather, yellow leather' six times fast.

- 'Gig whip' six times fast without any pause.

- 'She is a thistle sifter, and she has a sieve of sifted thistles and a sieve of unsifted thistles, because she is a thistle sifter.'

- 'The Leith police dismisseth us, and that sufficeth us.'

- 'He generally reads regularly in a government library particularly rich in Coptic manuscripts, except during the month of February.' Sound every syllable.

- Transcendentalism, existentialism, congratulatory, interpretively, supererogation, argumentativeness, latitudinarianism, macrodiagonalistic, intercommunicability.

EXERCISE IN RESONANCE

- Enemy, enemy, many men, enemy.
- The murmuring of innumerable bees in immemorial elms.
- Many men have many minds.
- The man from Hong Kong was beating the gong, and it boomed and it thundered round Pal-en-jen-bang.

TELEPHONE TECHNIQUES

Most of us have to use the telephone at work either to respond to people's enquiries or to obtain information from others.

Very often the telephone is the only point of contact we have with our customers. How each of us treats callers will therefore affect the way in which our organisation is seen. The process does not stop with the telephonist — it continues with all of us whenever we answer our telephone.

Most of us would agree that we want to create an image of ourselves and of our organisation which is helpful, efficient and friendly. Unfortunately this does not always happen for a variety of reasons. Some of these are given below:

- not returning calls when you said you would
- not answering promptly
- eating, drinking, smoking on the telephone — it can all be heard
- leaving people hanging on without keeping them informed of what is happening
- not being prepared to tell the caller your name
- holding two conversations at once
- asking the caller to call back
- transferring people round and round the organisation
- unintelligible greetings or just saying *'hello'* when answering
- negative attitude
- sounding unsure of what you are saying

It is also far easier to be evasive, petulant and even rude on the telephone than it is when we are face to face with someone.

Because of the busy working lives most of us lead, it is also easy to see the telephone as an interruption. How frustrating it is when it rings when we are half way through adding a column of figures or writing a difficult letter. That irritation can be heard in our voice.

However much we feel this piece of machinery is a distraction, it is vital for continuing the prosperity of our organisation. Seventy per cent of new business is initiated over the telephone. Can any of us afford to leave things to chance?

Creating the right image on the telephone is helped by a number of factors:

- establishing a good telephone procedure in the organisation

- establishing consistency in the way the telephone is answered throughout the organisation

- including 'how to use the telephone' in induction sessions for all new employees.

There is no doubt that if everyone in the organisation adopts the right approach to the telephone, we will be seen as the efficient, friendly and helpful organisation we want to be.

COMMUNICATING OVER THE TELEPHONE

A simple definition of communication is

'The creation of understanding in someone else's mind, in order to promote action.'

Communication is a two-way process and the understanding we aim to create must be accurate in every way.

When we talk to people face to face we have the great advantage of being able to see them. This helps because we can actually see how they are responding to our message. We can easily recognise the 'glazed look' when someone has not quite grasped our meaning and we can act on that and try saying it in a different way until we are satisfied we have got the message across.

On the telephone we are hampered because all the visual contact has gone (at least until a telephone with a video screen is invented). We therefore have to rely on two crucial elements:

- listening and concentrating on what we hear

- our voice — the tone and the words we use.

LISTENING

When we are on the telephone to someone, we are either speaking or listening. We often regard speaking as an active process and listening as a passive one. However, **listening well** can be a lot more difficult than speaking, and requires a lot more effort.

On the telephone it is just as easy to stop listening, for various reasons:

- having pre-conceived ideas about what the caller is going to say

- something distracting us in the office

- the caller having an uninteresting voice

- panicking because of our own inexperience.

One of the best solutions to poor listening is to concentrate our minds on the subject matter by taking notes. Have a telephone pad and pen next to the telephone at all times and if necessary fix them in some way to the desk so they do not get lost. There is nothing more frustrating than scrabbling around for something to write on or with after the call has started. Taking notes right from the beginning of the conversation saves repeating small but vital facts later on and minimises the effect of distractions going on around us.

Finally we need to make sure the caller knows that we are listening. When speaking face to face we use many non-verbal signs to indicate this, such as nodding. On the telephone we need to use **'verbal nods'**. For example, we need to say *'I see'*, *'yes'*, *'okay'*, *'right'* or *'mmm'* to indicate:

- that we are still there, and

- that we are listening.

VOICE

As we have no visual contact on the telephone we cannot use non-verbal body signs to help attract and keep the listener's attention; we have only *our voice*. However, it is not just what we say (words) but the way we say it (tone) that is important in creating the right image. We need to capitalise on these two elements to make up for the loss of visual contact.

Words are the tools of a speaker's trade and we should bear the following points in mind if we are to be successful. Use words which

- form pictures in the mind of the listener. For example, instead of saying *'hold on'* and disappearing, try *'I need to check that in our files, but it shouldn't take a moment.'*

- are jargon free and pitched at the level of the caller. A typical example follows:

  Caller: *"Can I speak to your Accounts Department?"*
  Us: *"Is it bought ledger or sales ledger you want?"*

  Since most people do not know the difference we should reply

  "Yes, what is it in connection with?"

- are not colloquial or too familiar. Avoid things like 'Guv' or 'lovie'. Show respect to the caller.

- are positive and helpful. Avoid negatives like *'busy'*, *'try'* and *'don't know'*. Instead try *'I will find someone who can help you,'* or *'Can I call you back in ten minutes when I have found the answer?'*

Tone of voice conveys the way we are feeling about the conversation, the caller or the way we feel on that particular day. The following positive and negative emotions can all be conveyed by our voice:

- enthusiastic or bored

- tired or alert

- aggressive or calm

- confident or unsure

One good way of making sure we sound right is to smile when we are talking. Smiling relaxes the vocal chords and has a dramatic effect on the voice, instantly making us sound more friendly and relaxed.

It is, however, crucial that when the phone rings we try and put everything out of our mind and concentrate on the person on the other end of the phone. In this way we can avoid sounding harassed, annoyed, or conveying any number of negative emotions.

We need to adopt the right approach to using the telephone before we start. We need to listen carefully and adopt a positive and professional approach in our choice of words and the way we sound. **And don't forget to smile!**

DEVELOPING TELEPHONE SKILLS

When we answer the telephone, we are the organisation, and developing good skills will help make sure that people will want to deal with our organisation and us personally in the future.

The only difference between a business call and calling a friend for a chat is that with the business call there is usually a specific purpose to be achieved.

To achieve the purpose of the call there are three main areas which need consideration:

- preparing for the call

- controlling the call

- following up action agreed after the call has finished.

PREPARING FOR CALLS

We may think we can prepare nothing in advance before picking up the telephone when it rings. However, to provide an efficient service there is a lot of background work needed.

For receiving calls we need all the following:

- a good knowledge of our organisation, its products or services and our colleagues. It is difficult when we first start in a job to know all this but to some extent we must find out ourselves. We should try to

  - read brochures on our organisaton
  - meet and get to know as many people as possible and what they do in the organisation
  - find out thoroughly what happens in our own department or section.

- an up-to-date internal telephone directory. This again can be usefully cross-referenced to particular functions and alternative people if one number is engaged.

- a pad and pen fixed near the phone. A simple message pad can be useful. The rules for message-taking are given later in this chapter.

- our organisation's brochures if we are involved in informing customers about our products and services.

A good way to add to our background knowledge is simply to ask our colleagues lots of questions. If we do not know the answer to a caller's request, we should not simply transfer the call to someone else. We should also find out the answer ourselves later, so we will be able to help next time.

CONTROLLING CALLS

There are a number of golden rules which apply to all incoming calls, whether from within the organisation or from outside.

ANSWER PROMPTLY

There is nothing worse when ringing someone than to hear the phone ring for ages. A good standard is three or four rings. This rule applies to other people's telephones when they are not there. It is not enough to assume you will not be able to help — think of the person at the other end — they would rather hear a voice than end up putting the phone down in frustration.

GIVE A GREETING

This should consist of:

> *'Good morning/afternoon*
> *Our Department*
> *Our name'*

e.g.: *'Good morning, Accounts Department, Felicity Brown speaking.'*

From this greeting, the caller can identify whether they are through to the right department and also have a friendly voice quite happy to say who they are. Interestingly enough, when we answer like this, callers respond immediately by telling us their name. This is useful to acquire early on because we can then use that person's name throughout the call, i.e.

'I'll make sure you receive the information by tomorrow, Mr Jones.'

This again sounds tremendously friendly and helpful.

USE APPROPRIATE QUESTIONS TO MAINTAIN CONTROL

There are basically two types of questions — open and closed. Open questions are those which require more than a straight 'yes' or 'no'. They begin with — who, where, when, how, why, what. Closed questions, conversely, require a 'yes/no' answer. They generally start — did you, was it, have you, etc. We need to use the appropriate questioning techniques to elicit the relevant information from the caller, i.e.

'Did you want more information on that?' may just get *'yes'*. *'What more information would you like on that?'* You will get specifics.

KEEP PEOPLE INFORMED

If for any reason we have to leave our caller holding on, it is crucial that we keep them informed of what is happening. We should tell them how long we will be and if appropriate offer to call them back with the information they require.

NEVER HOLD TWO CONVERSATIONS

It doesn't matter what else is happening in the office, even if our boss is breathing down our neck, the person on the other end of the phone deserves our sole attention, so try to ignore everything else but the caller.

Be with you in a minute Mr Jones.... Anyway I says to our Brenda...

CHECK ALL DETAILS

Names, phone numbers, addresses and any other details should always be repeated back to the caller to make sure we have got it right.

SUMMARISE ACTION

A useful way of closing the call is to summarise to the caller what is going to happen next, e.g.

'I will make sure our Accounts Department contacts you by Monday.'
'I will send you our catalogue in the post tonight.'
'If you could post the details to me tonight, first class post, I will make sure you have our proposal by Friday.'

It is important in the summary to set deadlines for when any action must happen. Of course, having done that we must make sure we stick to that deadline. Nothing sounds more haphazard than

'I'll let you have the information sometime next week.'

TRANSFERRING CALLS

If you have ever been transferred round and round an organisation, having to repeat your story, you will know what a frustrating experience this is. By following the guidelines below we can ensure our callers are dealt with efficiently.

- Know your telephone system thoroughly. With the varied or different telephone systems available we need to know which buttons to press to transfer calls.

- Tell the caller what is happening. Tell them the name and extension number of the person you are transferring them to, so that if they do get cut off they can get back to the right person.

- When you have got the person you wish to transfer the call to on the line, give them the relevant information. Don't just put the call through saying nothing. Tell them the caller's name, company and request briefly.

- If you receive a transferred call you can, armed with the information above, greet the caller thus:

  'Good afternoon, Mr Taylor, Susan Brown here. I understand you need some information on word processing software.'

  This sounds much better than simply, *'Hello, can I help you?'*

- If the person we wish to transfer the call to is engaged or unavailable we should give the caller options on how to proceed:

  - to hold until the person is free

    – to leave a message with you for the right person to ring back.

- If the caller opts to hold, keep going back to them to tell them what is happening. Do give them a chance to reply. If the wait becomes lengthy, they may decide to ring back later.

FOLLOW-UP ACTION AFTER THE CALL

The most important point here is that we ensure the things we promised do happen.

If we said someone else will ring the caller back we must make sure that they do. Unfortunately if this does not happen, it leaves the caller with the impression of inefficiency.

MAKING CALLS

We can often prepare much more thoroughly before we make a telephone call ourselves, and here it is just as important to remember our aim of being helpful, friendly and efficient.

There are various stages:

- Identify the purpose of the call clearly. We must clear our minds thoroughly before we start.

- If we have various things we wish to cover it is wise to make some notes to make sure nothing has been missed. If necessary we should devise a simple record pad.

- Consider the time of day we are making the call. There are two reasons for this. Calls in the UK are cheaper after 1.00 pm. It is a good idea therefore to plan to make all but urgent outgoing calls in the afternoon.

Secondly, we need to consider the person we are calling. A lengthy call at 4.45 pm on a Friday afternoon may not be well received. Certainly if we are making calls abroad we need to make sure the person we want will actually be at work because of the time differences.

DIFFICULT CALLS

Many things can go wrong during a telephone call — some are due to difficult people and some are quite simply caused by mechanical problems. Both types of difficulties need to be approached professionally. The points below may help to overcome some of the most common problems.

Many telephone systems have lots of special functions enabling us to store telephone numbers in a memory, programme the telephone to keep dialling a number until we get through, and so on. Many of these functions can help us so we need to familiarise ourselves with the scope (or limitations) of our system.

There are mechanical difficulties, however, with all telephones that are somewhat out of our control, for example:

- crossed lines

- being cut off

- bad lines where we cannot hear the other person clearly

- wrong numbers

Let us look at these in more detail and consider the best way of dealing with them if they arise.

CROSSED LINES

We can usually tell when someone dials in on our call. Often the dialling makes it impossible for us to continue speaking. When the interference stops, we should establish whether anyone else is on the line by saying: *'I think we have a crossed line'* and by suggesting, politely, that they should redial.

BEING CUT OFF

It is generally accepted that if we get cut off, the person who initiated the call should redial. However, if it is an important client and we have their telephone number, it is a good idea to ring them back. Then, when we start the conversation again, we should avoid getting bogged down discussing whose fault it was that we got cut off.

BAD LINES

If a line really is bad, it is better to explain as clearly as possible that we will call back.

WRONG NUMBERS

Even if we have dialled the right number, we can sometimes find ourselves through to the wrong one. If in doubt, we should ask the other person if they are the 'XYZ Company' and give them the number we dialled. We should not expect them to tell us their number. Since there are many odd calls which people get, particularly at home, many of us are reluctant to tell apparent strangers our telephone number.

DIFFICULT CALLERS

Apart from these obvious mechanical problems, we can face a lot of other difficulties with the callers themselves.

Probably the caller we all most dread is the rude, aggressive person who more often than not is complaining about something. Apart from the need to remain professional in the face of extreme adversity, the following tips are also crucial:

• Accept responsibility for whatever is being complained about. You are the organisation to the caller, and there is nothing worse than saying things like *'It's always happening, this sort of thing'* or *'Yes, they're hopeless in that section'* or worse still, *'You're the tenth person this week who's complained about that.'*

- Apologise

- Avoid taking any insults personally. Often people complaining just want to get it off their chest and once they have calmed down we can deal with the problem constructively.

- Finish the call positively by telling the caller what will happen next.

- Take follow-up action immediately and make sure you ring back if you said you would.

Efficient handling of complaints can often result in a pleased and impressed customer who will come back to us again.

Three other techniques can also be useful if dealing with difficult callers.

COULD IT BE MRS. SMITHSON-BURGOYNE?

QUESTIONS

Using the right combination of open and closed questions can determine the type of response we get. For example if we have a caller who does not seem to be able to get to the point, asking open questions could make the situation worse. If we ask a series of closed questions we may get to the purpose of the call more quickly.

ALTERNATIVES

Offering alternatives to the caller can sometimes help us as well as them. If, for example, we cannot get the information a caller wants, saying *'would you like to hold on, or shall I call you back?'* can help. Callers can then decide for themselves, rather than our deciding for them.

USING THE CALLER'S NAME

As we have said already, giving our name when we answer the phone immediately prompts callers to give us theirs.

Using the caller's name is a good way of interrupting. If we have a rather vague, waffly caller, by the interjection of — *'Mrs Lewis, did you send the goods back?'* we can get the caller's attention and follow-up with a closed question to keep control of the call.

Finally, the most important thing to do when dealing with difficult callers is to treat them as we would like to be treated if we were them, i.e. **politely and efficiently.**

TAKING MESSAGES

We have devoted an entire chapter to this activity. One of the major complaints from people at work in this whole area is that people simply do not ring back.

Unfortunately, if we take a message for someone and they do not ring back it is our fault, and that is how the caller will see it. They will probably assume the message was not passed on and they will therefore blame us.

So, how can we ensure that messages are dealt with promptly and efficiently?

There are three stages to effective message taking, all equally important.

- Being prepared.

- Taking the message.

- Making sure it is dealt with.

BEING PREPARED

At the outset, it must be said that offering to take a message is the lowest form of help. We should only offer to do this when we have explored all the other avenues. Many people, when answering someone else's phone simply say: *'I'm sorry he's out, can I take a message?'* That is not helpful. Instead we should say:

'I'm sorry, he is out. Can I help at all?' and very often we can, and the call is dealt with there and then.

However, for those occasions when we do have to take a message, we should be armed with a suitable message pad.

It is important to use a special pad or form, otherwise important messages get lost among the papers on someone's desk. It is preferable to have them printed on coloured paper, so they stand out.

Many people design their own pads and have them duplicated, so they can make sure the right information is received.

TAKING THE MESSAGE

We have already said that if we take down any information like telephone numbers, names and so on, we should repeat them to the caller to make sure they are correct.

We should also note down what action we have said will be taken. If we have said someone will call back this afternoon, we must make sure that the person dealing with the message both knows and does that.

Finally, make sure the person you are passing the message onto can read your writing.

MAKING SURE THE MESSAGE IS ACTIONED

Having taken the message, the next step is to make sure something happens about it. It is important, therefore, to leave it in a prominent place where it will be seen. Many organisations have message boards in each department or section so that all messages can be pinned up. Certainly, try to avoid just adding your message to someone's in-tray. It may get covered by incoming post.

If you are going to be out of the office for any length of time, tell either the switchboard or a colleague who sits nearby how long you will be. This will help them to deal with your calls efficiently. Above all if you receive a message — do carry out the action promised.

THE ROLE OF THE TELEPHONIST

The telephonist's role in creating the initial impression of the organisation is absolutely crucial. The importance of the telephonist cannot be overstressed. We have already looked at the way other staff should answer calls — the same rules apply to the telephonist.

Say *'good morning/afternoon'* first, followed by the name of the organisation and perhaps *'may I help you?'* The smile in the voice is vital here. Because the telephonist is so important to the organisation it is also wise to help that person do his or her job well. Every organisation can do this by laying down the ground rules that must be adhered to.

For example:

- Give priority to incoming calls.

- Give a clear greeting (as above).

- Tell the caller that they are being put through
  e.g. *'Putting you through'* or
  'It's ringing for you.'

- Reassure waiting callers they are not forgotten.

- If the extension is engaged or not being answered ask if you can put them through to another in the same department or someone who can take a message.

- Be helpful and friendly — the caller is relying on you.

- Listen carefully and be responsive.

- Don't tell callers through the tone of your voice, or in actual words, how many calls there are so you can't spend time with them. If you control the call with effective questions, that will cut down the time wasted considerably.

PRACTICAL AIDS FOR THE TELEPHONIST

It is most important that the telephonist should have up-to-date information about the organisation. Make sure you know or have for quick and easy reference the following information:

- Names and locations of the chairman, managing director, executives, managers, their deputies and secretaries.

- All departments and their functions — so that help can be offered immediately to a vague enquirer and he or she can be put through to the right person.

GAINING COOPERATION FROM EXTENSION USERS

The relationship between telephonists and extension users is not always as it should be. In some organisations it is almost tradition to complain about telephonists — easy targets who are often situated in an isolated place, unknown by name to many staff and unable to answer their accusers.

Ideally, telephonists should be able to explain in person to extension users how they can help to provide an efficient service. This would be useful to include in the induction programme of new employees. If this is not possible, and even if it is, instructions from the telephonist can be listed alongside instructions on how to use your extension. Some points you might include are:

- Telephonist's priority is to answer incoming calls, please be patient if you need the telephonist for any reason during the particularly busy periods of 10.00–11.30 and 14.00–15.30.

- Please inform the telephonist if there is not going to be anybody in your office during a certain period and where calls should be directed, or programme your phone to automatically transfer to someone who will take messages if you are leaving the office. But remember to tell whomever it is that you are doing this.

- Please look up your own numbers wherever possible.

- Let the telephonist know if someone has:
  - changed their job/responsibilities within the organisation
  - left
  - changed their extension number
  - or is about to join the organisation.

- Please inform the telephonist of temporary staff working in the building and of their extension numbers.

If the telephonists do not have all the information they need, it is important to go and find out.

INTERVIEWING

The objective of this chapter is to set out some clear, practical guidelines for anyone about to conduct an interview. The general section deals with skills which are needed for all types of interviews — individual sections look in more depth at each different type of situation:

- selection interviews (page 81)
- counselling interviews (page 92)
- grievance interviews (page 98)
- disciplinary interviews (page 105)
- appraisal interviews (page 109)
- termination interviews (page 115)

WHAT IS AN INTERVIEW?

This chapter is based on the assumption that the following definition describes an interview:

> **'A meeting of persons for discussion where there is an explicit objective to the conversation, and where one party is responsible for achieving this objective.'**

In other words, when we are interviewing we are conducting a type of conversation, with a purpose. The important point, however, is that we are responsible for controlling this conversation — and achieving the purpose. This is the job of the interviewer.

WHY NOT PLAY IT BY EAR?

Imagine learning to play snooker. There will be no substitute for experience — players who have been competing for ten years will have obvious advantages over you. But players who have not only got ten years of their own experience, but have exchanged 'tips' with two other players with ten years behind them, have the benefit of 20 years' experience at their finger tips as opposed to players who refuse to listen to others. Similarly, a newcomer can spend ten years learning these skills the hard way but can also ask more experienced players for advice. It may take a further ten years to develop a brilliant winning style — but the immediate results will be a great deal better for the application of a few simple rules. 'Playing it by ear' is a very lengthy and haphazard way of learning in interviewing as well as in snooker. A good interviewer will not only learn from his or her own experience, but also look to others for skills that have been used and seen to be effective for years. This book aims to pass on some of those well-used and effective tips which have come from those with years of experience.

OBJECTIVE

It is essential for the interviewer to be well aware of the objective of the interview to be conducted. We cannot control and plan the interview if we do not know what we are aiming at; nor can we have any clear idea as to whether or not we have achieved our objective if we were not sure what it was. Interviewers without objectives are like motorists without destinations. Like motorists they may have the vehicle to get them there (the interview) and a map with which to guide them (an interview plan), but neither of those is any good without a final destination or objective. Motorists may find the place they are looking for eventually by accident as many interviewers achieve the unrecognised objective occasionally. However, more often than not, both the motorist and interviewer will go round and round in circles aimlessly!

The objective of an interview can determine the whole approach to the meeting. It is therefore important to start by looking at the types of interviews covered by this book, and the objective(s) of each.

Type of interview	Objective(s)
Selection	To select the best person available for the job and the circumstances surrounding it. To help candidates decide whether the job and circumstances are right for them.
Counselling	To listen to problems that may directly or indirectly affect the individual's work. To help the individual to solve or come to terms with the problem where possible.
Grievance	To enable the person to air complaints to discover the causes of dissatisfaction and where possible to remove them.
Disciplinary	To inform of, and correct, mistakes or bad behaviour by helping the person to improve — thus preventing the situation from arising again.
Appraisal	To appraise a person's performance over a given period in order to: ● assess performance, building on strengths and identifying needs and areas of difficulty ● identify areas for improvement, ways of overcoming weaknesses and consequent training needs ● discuss potential for development

Termination
- To discover a person's real reason for resigning, in order to prevent others from leaving and as feedback on recruitment success
- To secure the employee's goodwill by wishing them well
- Sometimes — to persuade individuals to change their minds

PREPARATION

Most interviews are a great deal more successful if some preparation has been made. Obviously, there are some situations where it is very difficult to do any planning — when someone drops in unexpectedly for a chat about a problem for instance. Generally, there are three types of preparation we ought to consider.

MENTAL

What is the objective?
How long should it last?
What do I know about the interviewee?
What approach should I adopt? (having taken into account the objective and knowledge of interviewee)

ENVIRONMENT

What sort of room do I use? (if there is a choice)
How should we sit? (over a desk, round a coffee table, in smoking area)

Are there any distractions? e.g.:
- sun in eyes
- wobbly chair
- no ashtray
- no table to put coffee cup on
- interesting view
- noise in general
- interruptions (telephone, people)

MATERIAL

What information do I need? e.g.:
- company rules
- personal files
- application form
- relevant statistics
- names of specialists
- limits of own authority
- job description

CONVERSATION AND CONTROL SKILLS

A good interviewer will use conversational skills to control the progress of the discussion, to make sure there is a common understanding and to elicit the necessary information.

QUESTIONING

Asking the right questions is half the battle in getting the required answers. Think before phrasing a question and ask yourself which is the most effective way of asking it.

The following types of questions will be useful:

Type of question	Example	Usage
OPEN	'Why did you decide to join the snooker club?'	These are questions that cannot be answered 'yes' or 'no'. They encourage the interviewee to expand and do more talking. It often elicits feelings and attitudes as well as facts. To be sure of asking an open question — remember always to prefix it with why? who? when? what? where? or how?
CLOSED	'I understand from what you've been saying that you like snooker. Is that right?'	A question to be answered YES or NO. This question summarises, and can bring the conversation back on to course if it has wandered. It enables the interviewer to tie up one part and move on to the next. It also helps to check mutual understanding quickly. Can be used to try to quieten the garrulous interviewee — but often does not succeed!
SPECIFIC	'On what day did you join the snooker club?'	Asks for specific information. There is only one correct answer to a specific question. Try using a lot of specific questions on a talkative interviewee or a 'waffler'. This is the only way of being sure of getting the facts you need — ask direct.

Type of question	Example	Usage
REFLECTIVE	'I find it difficult to know in what order to pot the colours.' 'Pot the colours?'	Reflects a statement or question by rephrasing it and sending it back to the other person. This technique keeps the interviewee talking and often giving more information in depth on a subject they have just finished talking about. It also avoids personal involvement or bias on the part of the interviewer if a direct question is asked of him or her which it is not wise to answer.
LEADING	'I think it's disgraceful that the snooker club has closed down, don't you?'	Here the required answer is indicated in the question. It is bad if used inadvertently. It only reinforces the interviewer's own ideas and provides no information about the interviewee. However, it can be well used as a test question to check a person's knowledge and attitudes. It can also be used an an easy question in the initial stages of the interview for a very nervous or young person — to settle them in.
HYPOTHETICAL	'If the snooker club were to close, what would you do?'	Good for use in selection interviewing — to test out reactions and speed of thinking — dealing with problems.

Type of question	Example	Usage
BEHAVIOURAL	'Tell me how you dealt with that tricky situation?'	Asks about past experience, as an indication that future behaviour might be similar under similar circumstances.

A good interviewer will alternate the questions to develop the appropriate style of interview. In most interviews, the interviewer needs to obtain both facts and feelings/attitudes, so a combination of open and specific questions is normally needed.

LISTENING AND OBSERVING

Listening to the answers is as important as phrasing the question well in the first place. It is only by listening that we can work out what our next question should be. Often, we have not received enough information or suspect that there is something odd about the answer. Here we need to probe the last answer further — not merely go on to the next step. We need to have been listening and observing very closely to pick up the clues. We have three channels of understanding in a face-to-face encounter:

- language — the actual meaning of the words

- tone of voice — the way it is said

- body movements — physical reaction while speaking.

Each of these enables us to understand more clearly, and so we should be paying attention to all three. Analyse *what* is being said, how it is being used and watch for emphasis or contradiction by facial expression, gesture, posture and eye-contact. Listen for what is *not* said and probe, pick up general points for more detailed expansion and notice discrepancies.

In addition to the importance of the actual listening itself — there is also the very important factor of *being seen to be listening.* This is an important part of establishing and maintaining rapport and encouraging the interviewee.

Eye-contact is the major way in which we show that we are listening and if we spend less than 30 per cent of the time establishing eye-contact the other person feels cut off. On the other hand over 60 per cent can be uncomfortable for the interviewee — too much looking is aggressive and causes lack of confidence. If the other person appears to be reacting uncomfortably, look away; if you want to re-establish contact — look.

Most of us get the balance right in normal conversation naturally. The trouble with the interview is that we are all a bit nervous and so tend often to react unnaturally. However, remember to keep looking even if the interviewee rarely looks at you.

STATEMENTS

The more talking the interviewer does, the less the interviewee can do. So there should be no talking for the sake of it, but sometimes we need to supply necessary information to direct the interview. We should make statements only if they achieve one of the following:

- *clarifying misunderstandings* that the interviewee might have

- *giving information* to enable the interviewee to understand the situation

- sometimes, making *statements of reassurance* to the interviewee (only necessary in certain circumstances).

SUMMARIES

A good interviewer uses both interim and final summaries when interviewing.

- *interim* — to keep control of the interview — to bring the conversation 'back on line'. To point out clearly where the interview has been and where it is going to enable both parties to keep track of progress.

- *final* — to give a good positive finish and to make clear the final and future action to both parties.

NOTE TAKING

All interviews require some form of written record. Explain at the outset that you will be taking notes and encourage the interviewee to do likewise. Selection interviewing notes are best kept to yourself; during most other types of interview it is good to let the interviewee know what you are writing, especially, for example, during the appraisal interview.

RAPPORT

All these skills will enable us to interview more successfully. However, all the skills in the world will not help us if we cannot establish some sort of relationship with the interviewee. Establishing rapport is not just a question of a joke, some aimless chatter and a quick cup of coffee; indeed in a discipline interview this would be totally inappropriate. It is much more a case of having the right approach to the interviewee. This approach should be positive, purposeful, but permissive.

- We should assure the interviewee that we are in control of the interview by directing its course throughout (this gives the interviewee the confidence that something is to be achieved as a result of the interview).

- Make sure that the purpose of the interview is quite clearly stated together with some guidance on how the interview will proceed towards that goal (this gives the interviewee confidence of learning *what* is to be achieved and how).

- Despite the above two points, we should not, as interviewers, monopolise the interview, but encourage the interviewee to talk freely and relax by using encouraging smiles, nods and comments (this gives the individual freedom within the secure framework of a well-controlled interview).

BE INTERESTED

Relaxation and common understanding can be difficult to achieve, but are essential in order to break down any communication barriers that may prevent the interview from succeeding. There is no substitute for genuine interest and concern on the part of the interviewer towards the interviewee. We have all experienced the feeling of hopelessness when talking to someone who is not interested or cannot be bothered. The odd yawn, quick look at the clock, the glazed look, the *'I've only got two minutes . . .'* How do you feel? Cut off?

DEVELOP EMPATHY

Become interested in the other person. Try to develop empathy — an understanding of the other person's feelings in a situation — and you will become involved and communicate more clearly in the process.

GENERAL INTERVIEWING CHECKLIST

OBJECTIVE

What am I to achieve by the end of this interview?

PREPARATION

What can I do, if anything, before the interview under the three headings:

- mental

- environment

- material

> **SKILLS**
>
> What can I do during the interview to stimulate communications but retain control? Am I
>
> - questioning efficiency
> - listening and observing
> - making statements when necessary
> - using summaries
> - taking notes
> - establishing and maintaining rapport?
>
> **FOLLOW-UP**
>
> Have I taken any action, if there was any agreed on at the close of the interview? If not — when do I need to take action by?

1. THE SELECTION INTERVIEW

The penalties for selecting badly are enormous. They can include any one or more of the following:

COST

A large company in the south of England recently calculated the average cost of recruitment for their staff. This included not only the cost of advertising, but the cost of their training to do the job and other 'invisible' costs — it came to over £20,000 per person. If we choose the wrong people and they leave because they cannot do the job then we incur the cost of another recruitment. That is in addition to loss of time we have incurred in having to start again.

This is not an argument for keeping a person on if they cannot do the job, however. Certainly, we will not have the cost of recruitment to pay — but the cost of keeping an underproductive person in a job may well prove far more expensive in the long term and can also cause:

TEAM PROBLEMS

When a group of people work as a team, a person not pulling their weight adds pressure to the rest of the group. Often, this causes resentment and good members of the department or section leave as a result. It may equally result in low morale in the group and an overall lowering of work standards. The problem need not necessarily be one of inability to do the job. It is very common to hear of individuals being employed who are extremely good at doing the job — but whose personalities clash with that of the rest of the group. This also causes low morale and often resignations.

Cost and team achievement are not the only problems resulting from poor recruitment, but even these are rarely considered seriously. It is common to hear managers say: *'I haven't got time to prepare for this interview, I've more important things to do.'* Selection interviewing is one of the most important jobs a manager can do, and should not be treated as *'something that has to fit in with the usual routine, but is not really part of my job.'* The responsibility is ours and no-one else's. The success of an organisation depends upon the sum of its individual employees' work — every misplaced individual detracts from that success.

OBJECTIVE

The objective of a selection interview is straightforward. It is to select the best person available for the job and the circumstances surrounding it. There are, however, two secondary objectives at this interview

- To help candidates decide whether the job and circumstances are right for them

- To give a good impression of the organisation to the outside world

A selection interview is, to some extent, a public relations exercise. Those accepted and those not accepted for jobs all leave with an impression of the organisation. That impression is largely derived from us, as interviewers; we are the company as far as the interviewee is concerned. It does not take long for a bad reputation to develop either in the local district or within the same industry or business.

PREPARATION

Preparation is crucial. Much of the success of a selection interview depends on thorough preparation. This need not take hours, just good planning. For instance, six interviews for one job do not entail going through all the preparatory steps six times — only the application forms and interview plans need studying before each one.

It is important to be clear about what the job involves and what sort of person could fill it. From a comparison of the application form with this information, an interview plan can be sketched out to expand and supplement the information on it. This should be a list of areas needing to be covered rather than an inflexible time-table. It is important as a checklist during the interview — it is surprising how often the simpler questions slip the mind during the anxiety of the occasion . . . *'I don't need a plan — I know all about this job and I know what I'm looking for'* sounds marvellous before the interview, but often leaves the interviewer desperately searching for something to say during the interview itself. Very few people are spontaneously good — most of us would be rather arrogant and foolhardy to rely on spontaneous genius emerging! We need therefore to prepare the following:

- job description (a written picture of the job to be filled)

- person specification (a written picture of the person needed to do the job)

- application form (how does it compare with the above?)

- interview plan (headings of areas needing discussion or answers) plus specific questions to be asked (see under 'Rapport')

- assessment system (some way of assessing one candidate against another)

- company information (company structure, other locations, products, pensions, sick pay, social club, loans and conditions of service, etc.)

- environment (will the candidate be greeted at reception, is the room lay-out suitable, is tea/coffee arranged, can interruptions be minimised or stopped etc?)

- relevant legislation — do I know about it?

SKILLS

- ask open questions to get the conversation going and to encourage the interviewee to talk

- make sure that all the facts are drawn out by using specific questions

- start with an easy leading question if the candidate is shy or retiring

- have any hypothetical questions ready prepared before the interview starts. These are invaluable in the selection interview to test how the individual would think through and approach a problem. It also tests the person's knowledge. Ask these sorts of questions when the interviewee has 'settled in' — later rather than sooner — they can be nerve-racking

- ask questions to get a balanced view — no-one is perfect all the time.

PROBE

Never accept a partial answer or one that dodges the question — probe the answer for more details. If you are suspicious of an answer, probe by asking it again in a different guise — you may find out more.

LISTEN

It is only if we listen carefully that we can probe effectively. We need to pick up inconsistencies and delve more deeply. Watch and listen both to what is said and how it is said. Use 'pregnant' pauses, do allow the interviewee to think and reply.

USE NOTES

There is a quotation which says 'A short pencil is more effective than a long memory.' Most of us find listening difficult and remembering what we have heard, harder. A quick note will remind us of interesting points or inconsistencies we have picked up that need probing later. If we do not jot this down, the chances are that we will remember what we meant to ask when the person has gone.

Apart from this, notes are essential as a record. This is especially so if there are four or five or more people to be seen. How can we assess them with any sort of objectivity if we cannot remember what they had to say and what we felt about it? If a case of discrimination is brought against us, how can we show that we did not unfairly discriminate if we cannot say why we preferred one person against another? Notes should be kept for at least six months after the interview for this reason.

Notes can distract the interviewee if they are not taken carefully, but the following points will help us to avoid this:

- always ask interviewees at the outset if they mind your taking notes (many people actually take this as a compliment)

- do not try to take down everything — just jot down the key words or facts

- try to sit so that the candidate cannot see what you are writing

- make a point of writing down notes when the interviewee is highlighting information that *they* thinks is important

- do not write down a bad point immediately, the interviewee will feel it may be no use going on!

Wait until another good point arises and write them both down together

- maintain eye-contact — do not allow the notes to become more interesting than the person.

STATEMENTS

Make sure that the interviewee has all the information about the job/company. Be honest, if the job is in a room with 20 other people and there are no windows — let this be known. It is better to lose the candidate at the interview than to appoint somebody and have them leave within a few months of joining.

On the other hand, there is little to be gained by exaggeration of the problem — it may sound so much like the black hole of Calcutta that nobody would want to work there! In this sort of case it is a good idea to supplement statements about the job with a walk around the place of work.

SHOWING CANDIDATES THE WORK AREA

If this is possible, it can be a very useful exercise. It has two advantages:

- If the candidate will not be happy or prepared to work in the environment, you can find that out on the spot, e.g.:
  A large company in west London interviewed a secretary for a job in their interview room on the ground floor. When she arrived for her first day at work, she was told she would be working on the twelfth floor. She was claustrophobic and could not use the lift! She left the same day.

●It is useful and often illuminating to introduce the person to other people in the department/section to see how they react to the individuals they could be working with.

SUMMARIES

Interim summaries will help to keep the discussion on track and to control a garrulous interviewee. A final summary leaves the candidate with a good impression of the company whether or not they are offered the job; it enables the interviewee to know what the next step is.

Before making a final summary, check that the interviewee has no further questions. Then:

●confirm the areas that have been covered during the interview

●ask if they would still be interested if they were to be offered the job

●let the candidate know when they will be contacted

●thank them for their time and interest in the job

●shake hands and show them out.

RAPPORT

This is crucial in the selection interview. Help the interviewee to relax as soon as possible. The length of time this will take depends very much on the age and experience of the candidate, and their own personal confidence. It may take two minutes with some and fifteen minutes with others, but launching into a barrage of questions will produce very limited results until the person is 'settled'. The following suggestions may help:

- **be positive** — give the interviewee the security of knowing that you are in control and are well-organised. Do this by explaining the objectives of the interviewee and by outlining the plan of the interview before it starts — so that the candidate knows what to expect. A good approach is **WASP**:

  Welcome — general chat about the company and job

  Ask — question about the candidate's experience

  Say — in more detail, what the job involves and take the candidate's questions

  Parting — final summary and explain what happens next

- **be kind** — make sure that the room is suitable. Try to avoid interruptions by using forethought. Arrange for a cup of tea/coffee. Make sure that there is a table to put the drink down on. (The shaky hand does terrible things to a cup of tea.) Be prepared to give the candidate time to drink the tea! Check that the sun is not going to be in the candidate's eyes and that the chair is comfortable.

- **be interested** — even if it is the fifth candidate that day. Show interest by listening and eye-contact — give encouragement by smiling, nods, giving them a chance to talk freely, get up to meet them, smile and shake hands — show them to the chair. Start the conversation informally on an easy topic, e.g. the journey. Do not forget — people need several minutes to adapt to a new environment.

FOLLOW UP

• assess the candidates using a system. Guard against unnecessary bias

• do reply to the candidate within the time limit that you set at the end of the interview. All interviewees must be contacted after an interview. It is very distressing for an interviewee not to be informed as quickly as possible; it is also very unprofessional and so bad for the image of the company as a whole. If there are several possible candidates, do not send out rejections to the second and third choices until the first has accepted — you may still need them!

REFERENCES

Take up references if possible before making an offer of employment. Ring up or write to a *previous* employer — not the present one — and ask *specific* questions. Usually people are much more forthcoming on the telephone than in writing. A reference from the present company employer can be taken up after a conditional offer has been made. Statements such as *'Susan works well under close supervision'* should be considered carefully — often what is *not* said in a reference is more telling than what *is* said.

Finally — make arrangements for the individuals to start work (organise induction programme etc.).

SELECTION INTERVIEWING CHECKLIST

OBJECTIVE

To select the best person available for the job and the circumstances surrounding it. To help candidates decide whether the job and circumstances are right for them.

PREPARATION

- study all available information

    job description
    person specification
    application form
    test results
    school reports etc.

- make an interview plan (not a rigid timetable) and prepare questions

- allow adequate time

- check that the room is adequate and as free from interruptions as possible, arrange tea/coffee

- ensure proper reception for applicant

SKILLS

- welcome interviewee
- establish rapport
- encourage applicant to talk freely by asking open questions
- note important facts and thoughts
- listen, observe and probe
- check against plan that all areas are covered
- give information about the company and job
- check that the candidate gets a fair hearing and has no other questions
- advise when an answer can be expected

FOLLOW-UP

- decide on best applicant, guard against bias
- inform applicants of your decision
- arrange for new member of staff to start

2. THE COUNSELLING INTERVIEW

Counselling is a necessary part of any manager's or personnel officer's job. Problems may be related to people's work or their personal lives — both will affect the way they do their job.

OBJECTIVE

To listen to problems that may directly or indirectly affect the individual's work. To help the person to solve or come to terms with the problem where possible.

PREPARATION

Often preparation is not possible. People often 'pop-in' to talk about a problem without warning. In case this happens, it is a good idea always to have a list of specialists and their phone numbers handy. There are people to whom you can refer your member of staff, if the problem is beyond your own expertise, e.g.:

- Citizens Advice Bureau — CAB

- Local Authority (social services)

- Marriage Guidance Counsellor — Relate

- Family Planning Clinic

- Accounts department (to help with tax, money problems)
  If there is some time to plan ahead, try to:

- find a private place without interruptions

- allow plenty of time before next appointment

- check individual's file

- if you know what the problem is, check own limits of authority in dealing with it

- have some tissues handy (in case of tears).

SKILLS

Allow the individual to talk freely without interruptions. Put them at ease — reassure them that what is said will go no further — offer a cup of tea/coffee.

QUESTIONS

The objective of this interview is to help and 'advise' — not to tell the interviewee what you think they should do. The 'tell' approach is a bad one for two reasons:

- if the person acts on your word and things get worse, it will be seen as your fault!

- telling a person what to do does not help the person to solve the next problem when it comes along — you may become their permanent counsellor!

It is therefore better as a 'rule of thumb' to be asking questions rather than making statements during this type of interview.

OPEN QUESTIONS

Use these initially to start the person talking freely about the problem.

SPECIFIC QUESTIONS

Use these to get to the bottom of the problem as stated. Often the real problem when examined objectively is not the problem that the interviewee originally thought it was! Little advisory work can start until all the facts are revealed.

REVERSE QUESTIONS

Use these to encourage people to examine their own thoughts and statements, avoiding the commitment of yourself, e.g.:

> interviewee *'What do you think I can do?'*
> interviewer *'Well now, what do you think are things you could do?'*
> interviewee *'I don't know.'*
> interviewer *'Come on, are you telling me that you can't do anything?'*
> interviewee *'Well, I suppose I could either go on putting up with what my colleague's doing or leave.'*
> interviewer *'That's a rather all-or-nothing approach isn't it? Have you ever thought of talking it over with him or perhaps seeing his supervisor before making that sort of decision?'*

The aim of the questioning should be to help interviewees to think through alternatives that were not immediately apparent to them, and through that, to come to their own course of action. Prod but do not push!

LISTENING AND OBSERVING

The more talking the interviewer does, the less chance the interviewee has of sorting the problem out. The interviewee should be doing 90 per cent of the talking. It is only possible to give guidance and understanding if the interviewer listens and observes carefully throughout.

RAPPORT

Practise empathy — try to understand the other person's position and let them know that you do. Giving sympathy, however, can be most unproductive. Most people require a solid post to lean on, not somebody to wallow in the problem with them. Too much sympathy merely encourages interviewees to feel more sorry for themselves, concentrates on emotions rather than on a logical solution that will help.

Reassure the individual that the problem is important to you — many people are afraid of just being a nuisance and taking up your valuable time. Do not continually check your watch or the clock and try very hard to meet where there will be minimal interruptions.

Most important, make sure that the interview ends with some positive action to be taken. Summarise what action is to be taken at the end of the interview and make an appointment to see the person later to check what the results of that action were.

FOLLOW-UP

Always follow-up a counselling interview. Even if the problem was solved completely during the interview, make a point of asking the interviewee if everything is all right during the next few weeks. If the problem is a difficult one, actually make an appointment to have another meeting to talk about how things are going and what the next steps might be. Checking-up is important for three reasons:

- It assures the interviewee that you do care, and that you did not just forget about the whole thing after the interview.

- It encourages people to take action if they know that someone cares enough to find out about what has happened.

- It gives you feedback as to whether the problem has resolved itself or not and hence enables you to manage that person more effectively.

COUNSELLING INTERVIEW CHECKLIST

OBJECTIVE

To listen to problems that may directly or indirectly affect the individual's work. To help the person to solve or come to terms with the problem where possible.

PREPARATION

- keep a record of specialists who could give help

- ensure privacy and adequate time

- check limits of own authority

- look at individual's file

- plan approach according to the individual

SKILLS

- demonstrate understanding not sympathy

- ask open questions to encourage interviewee to talk freely

- reverse questions and statements to encourage person to come to terms with the problem

- listen and observe carefully throughout

- summarise with a positive conclusion and agreement of future action

FOLLOW-UP

- arrange for future interview to check developments

- carry out any action promised

3. THE GRIEVANCE INTERVIEW

A grievance is any dissatisfaction that employees have with the company or in their relationships with people who work for that company. The objective is similar to that of a counselling interview, although the emphasis is very different: in the counselling situation, advice is sought; in the grievance interview a complaint has been made. Ensure that you are not handling a grievance which should more properly be handled by someone else.

OBJECTIVE

To enable the person to air the complaint; to discover the causes of dissatisfaction and where possible to remove them.

PREPARATION

Often, the grievant arrives without any warning! In this case, obviously, preparation is not possible. However, 'keeping an ear to the ground' is often a good method of identifying potential grievants before they arrive at your door.

If there is a possibility that Fred may feel aggrieved — prepare for it just in case! Try to steer a grievant into a nearby quiet room if you are accosted in the corridor or in the department or on the shopfloor; it is difficult to talk freely with other people around, not to mention distractions and background noise.

Glad we sorted it out, Mr Perkins

If there is some warning of an approaching grievance, find out as much background *factual* information as is available. Check other people's feelings and attitudes as well, where they are relevant. Check records for any previous situations that were similar.

Make sure that you are clear about company policy and the limits of your own authority in dealing with the grievance. Especially make sure that you are clear about your grievance procedure, in case the person wishes to take the matter further.

Allow adequate time and ensure privacy where possible. Check to see whether the grievant is bringing a representative; inform the grievant of their right to do so, if it is part of the correct procedure.

SKILLS

Allow interviewee to get the grievance 'off their chest' as soon as possible. Once the grievance has been stated, ask questions to clarify the *exact* complaint. Sometimes the grievance is not as obvious as the interviewee first thinks that it is. There may be a deeper problem or problems underlying it, and this affair may have merely been 'the straw that broke the camel's back'. If this is the case, the interview may become a counselling one.

QUESTIONS

Start by asking the interviewee to outline the complaint in detail. Then:

- ask specific questions to clarify each point made

- use closed questions to check your understanding of the situation

- use hypothetical questions to try to help the interviewee to understand other people's point of view, e.g.:
  'If you were in Sally's position, Fred, how would you have felt?'
  'If you feel the system doesn't work as it is, Fred, how would you improve it?'

100

STATEMENTS

After the initial description of the grievance from the interviewee, re-state the complaint as you understand it. This makes absolutely sure that you have a clear picture of the situation. **Note it down.**

SUMMARIES

Summarise regularly throughout to make sure that you are clear about what has been said so far by both parties in order that the discussion is then moved on instead of going round in circles! **Note the main points.**

RAPPORT

Polite chat is not the way to establish rapport here. All interviewees are concerned about is telling you of a grievance — so let them. If people are very irate or upset, talking about it will settle them down; constant interruptions from the interviewer will cause further irritation. The most important first step is to try to get the grievant to sit down. It is difficult to maintain anger once seated.

EMOTION

It may be very daunting to be faced with anger or hysteria, but it is most important for the interviewer to set the atmosphere of calm reason. Do not be tempted to argue heatedly or become emotional yourself. Consciously avoid your natural emotional response. Once again it is not easy to be aggressive or hysterical for any length of time when the other person is calm and composed.

Do not commit yourself too quickly to any action.

LISTEN

Listen carefully and suggest appropriate solutions. Always finish the interview by stating what action is to take place as a result of the meeting. Above all, do not belittle an issue or try to evade it.

GRIEVANCE SOLVED

If you are able to settle the problem immediately, it is still important to see the person again to make sure that things have worked as planned. Sometimes nothing needs to be done at all. Merely talking about it, 'letting off steam', enables the person to accept a situation. Still, arrange to check back at a future date.

GRIEVANCE UNSOLVED

State what action you are going to take on the grievance; arrange a date by which to report results.

- If there is no action that you can take and the individual still feels aggrieved, point out the next step of the grievance procedure and arrange for the next meeting to take place — inform any union representatives of this if they are not at the meeting.

FOLLOW-UP

- Investigate facts and discover any other information needed

- Take any action necessary to solve the grievance

- Write up notes from the interview for the record

- Put grievance procedure into motion if necessary

- Follow-up the individual at a later date to check that all is going well.

GRIEVANCE INTERVIEW CHECKLIST

OBJECTIVE

To enable a person to air a complaint; to discover the causes of dissatisfaction and where possible remove them.

PREPARATION

- find out as much about the grievance as possible — facts, attitudes, feelings

- consult other people for advice

- check individual's file

- check for any previous situations that were similar

- confirm own limits of authority; check company policy

- be clear about the company grievance procedure
- allow for privacy and enough time
- find out if the individual is bringing a representative

SKILLS

- be calm but positive
- allow the grievant to 'let off steam' first
- check your mutual understanding of the exact situation and the facts
- listen carefully, probe deeply
- do not belittle the issue or dismiss it
- finish with positive action for the future. Make sure you are both sure of what happens next

FOLLOW-UP

- investigate facts and possible causes of action
- write notes
- follow-up interview
- take agreed action

4. THE DISCIPLINARY INTERVIEW

OBJECTIVE

To inform of, and correct mistakes or bad behaviour by helping the person to improve — thus preventing the situation from arising again.

PREPARATION

Start by being clear about the offence or short-comings in performance. Check all the facts carefully. However, try not to prejudge the outcome of the interview until you have heard what the interviewee has to say.

Try to plan the interview according to the individual concerned. Some people will be sensitive to the mildest criticism while others need a bomb behind them before they can appreciate the seriousness of the offence!

Consider carefully what sanctions are available to you and be quite clear about the stages of your disciplinary procedure. Also revise your knowledge of what your company handbook says on discipline. Look at ways in which the individual could be helped in the future. Finally, make quite sure that you can be private and have allowed enough time to deal with the problem. If the disciplinary procedure has been put into effect — advise interviewees that they may bring a representative. (If they are planning to do this, it is a good idea to have a back-up yourself.)

SKILLS

Establish the objective of the interview immediately. State the situation as you see it briefly and ask the interviewee to give their side of the story; do this by asking an open question.

QUESTIONS AND STATEMENTS

Ask specific questions to probe the facts of the matter and make statements to clarify standards of performance expected and company policy; make absolutely sure that the interviewee is fully aware of these.

RAPPORT

Keep calm, avoid arguments, but equally avoid being 'an easy touch'. Be firm but fair, e.g.:

THE 'EASY TOUCH'

Jane	*'I'm sorry I was late three times this week, but my car broke down so I couldn't help it.'*
Interviewer	*'Oh, all right then, let's forget it this time.'*

FIRM BUT FAIR

Jane	*'I'm sorry I was late three times this week, but my car broke down so I couldn't help it.'*
Interviewer	*'Well, Jane, I can understand that it was difficult on the first day; but I do feel that you should have found an alternative way of getting in by the second. Couldn't you have asked a neighbour to give you a lift? You could have caught the bus to get here on time if you had got up half-an-hour earlier than usual. We could have even arranged*

*for someone in the office to give you a lift on
their way in. I don't think you made very much
of an effort did you?'*

Where possible always point out to the interviewees
where their action has led to difficulties for colleagues.
The seriousness of letting a friend down is often
understood far more easily than that of letting the
company down, for example:

Interviewer   *'Do you realise Fred, that by arriving
half-an-hour late for your shift on Monday,
George had to work an extra half hour to cover
for you? That can't be very fair on him when
he's already worked all night, can it? How would
you feel?'*

Listen carefully and note all the facts. Then decide on
future action:

- Is the employee to be given a warning and the
  disciplinary procedure to be started? If so explain
  this fully.

- Whether the answer is yes or no — what action is
  to be taken to help the individual to do better/avoid
  further mistakes?

- When is the person to be seen again — giving a
  reasonable time in which to improve/show that the
  same offence will not be committed again?

Make sure that at the close of the interview, future
action has been clearly understood by the interviewee.

Disciplinary interviews should be approached
according to the stage of procedure reached. An informal,
problem-solving approach is often best at the initial
stage. The atmosphere may need to become more formal
if disciplinary action continues towards the final stage.
Considerate handling at the initial stages often prevents the
procedure from having to go any further.

FOLLOW-UP

Write up notes immediately after the interview (see current employment legislation on unfair dismissal). Involve the union representative if your company has a negotiated disciplinary procedure. Record any warnings given and send copies to the individual. Make an appointment for a future interview to review behaviour/performance.

DISCIPLINARY INTERVIEW CHECKLIST

OBJECTIVE

To inform of and correct mistakes or bad behaviour by helping the person to improve — thus preventing the situation from arising again.

PREPARATION

- be clear about the reasons for seeing the person
- have all the facts
- try not to prejudge
- plan approach according to the individual
- consider sanctions available
- know the procedure and the company handbook
- ensure privacy
- let interviewees know that they are entitled to have a representative present

SKILLS

- establish the objective of the interview

- state the reason for asking the person in

- ask interviewees for their side of the story, asking an open question

- probe the information given

- clarify standards of performance and/or company policy

- keep calm, be firm but fair

FOLLOW-UP

- write up notes immediately and file (unfair dismissal)

- send out copies of any warnings given

- make appointment for follow-up interview

- take any action you agreed on to help the individual

5. THE APPRAISAL INTERVIEW

An appraisal interview, when conducted properly, yields benefits for individual employees, management and the company as a whole. Relations between manager and job holder are considerably improved as a result of the two-way communication in the interview.

On the other hand, a badly conducted interview can easily lead to mistrust and suspicion on the part of the interviewee, which leads to lack of co-operation and lack of interest at the interview.

OBJECTIVE

The interview often fails because the interviewer is mistaken about the objective. It is not '. . . *to fill in the form*' or '. . . *to tell the person where they went wrong*'. It is an exchange of information between both parties concerning the individual's performance over a given period of time. The objective is to:

- assess performance, building on strengths and identifying problem areas, and to use that information to improve performance in the coming year

- identify areas for improvement, ways to overcome weaknesses and consequent training needs

- discuss potential for development.

PREPARATION

It is most important for both the manager and the job holder to prepare for this interview.

Appraisees need to be given at least a week's notice of the appraisal taking place and should be asked to prepare by considering the following points:

- their own performance over the last 12 months, especially areas of achievement and problem areas

- any training required, or help in the job

- future ambitions and development of self and/or
  job

- your management — could they do more to help?

Many companies now send out appraisal preparation forms to help the interviewee to clarify thoughts before the meeting.

Interviewer needs to study the job description and standards of performance. If targets were set after the last appraisal (or during the last few months) these need to be checked, and results noted. Note points of strengths and areas of weakness for discussion.

Before the interview check that the room is private and that there will be no interruption if possible. Try to make the seating arrangements fairly informal.

SKILLS

It is most important to reassure the interviewee right at the start about the objective of the interview and its two-way nature.

QUESTIONS

After stressing the objective, start by asking the interviewee for their thoughts. Encourage them to start talking straightaway.

Ask open questions to find out how the person feels about the job. Use specific questions to find out facts about how the job has gone that year. Try not to use leading questions — this tends to result in the interviewee telling you what you want to hear, and not what they think. Try to use reflective questions to encourage the interviewee to expand on points.

STATEMENTS

Try to make statements about the person's performance *after* getting their view. There is a great danger that the 'tell' approach will cut off any contribution from the employee. Putting your view first can make interviewees feel that there is no point in putting their points over because you have already made up your mind. Try to add to the employee's points, rather than submerging them.

SUMMARIES

Summarise each point as it is dealt with and make a final summary emphasising conclusions and future action. Take notes throughout, but especially about future targets and actions.

LISTENING AND OBSERVING

One of the biggest mistakes of an appraisal is for the appraiser to do most of the talking. This is pointless. The interviewer must listen carefully in order to make the interview worthwhile. Remember the objective is not 'to tell them where they went wrong'. It is not a disciplinary interview.

RAPPORT

It is most important that the appraisee feels relaxed and has been assured that the interview is a worthwhile exercise. Keep the atmosphere positive. When poor performance has to be discussed, try to look at it in terms of 'how can we improve' rather than just acknowledging the problem. Try to maintain a level of informality so that it is more of a purposeful chat than an inquisition.

FOLLOW-UP

- complete the appraisal form and show it to the interviewee. Allow the interviewee to comment in writing and then sign the form

- make sure that any action agreed during the interview is taken — e.g. booking on training courses etc. Make sure that any action taken is also followed-up to check its usefulness

- set a date to set targets for the next year/few months.

APPRAISAL INTERVIEW CHECKLIST

OBJECTIVE

To appraise an employee's performance over a given period in order to:

- assess performance, building on strengths and identifying problem areas, and to use that information to improve performance in the coming year

- identify areas of improvement, ways of overcoming weaknesses and consequent training needs

- discuss potential for development

PREPARATION

- give appraisee time to prepare
- check job description and any targets set
- note strengths and weaknesses
- think of ways improvements could be achieved
- arrange for a private room, and an informal setting

SKILLS

- state objective — stress two-sided nature of the interview
- ask open questions to encourage the interviewee to talk
- use reflective questions to encourage expansion and self-criticism on the part of the employee
- make statements after hearing from the appraisee
- summarise points throughout and at the close
- listen and observe carefully
- hold a 'purposeful chat' rather than an 'inquisition'
- take notes, especially of actions

FOLLOW-UP

- complete forms
- take any action agreed
- set a date for targets to be set

6. THE TERMINATION INTERVIEW

People leave organisations for all sorts of reasons — these reasons can be very important to us, because they can tell us about:

- poor recruitment (a check on our selection interview)

- inadequate training

- unsolved grievances/problems (that might have been solved)

- company policy/salaries

- poor management/supervision

A termination interview serves more purposes than this, but how many of us make sure that we take care to hold them?

OBJECTIVE

- To discover a person's real reason for resigning, in order to prevent others from leaving and as feedback on recruitment success.

- To secure the employee's goodwill by wishing them well.

- Sometimes — to persuade an individual to change their mind.

PREPARATION

Check the letter of resignation and the reason it gives for leaving. Does it seem reasonable according to your knowledge of that person? Study the person's file and chat to people who may be able to give extra clues — workmates, friends.

Make sure that you talk in private without interruption — allow adequate time.

SKILLS

Explain the purpose of the interview at the outset. Keep it informal. Ask open questions to find out more facts than are given in the resignation letter. Often the reason stated is not the full story or even the real reason — but has been written for convenience.

Listen and observe carefully. Often a resignation is a final cry for help or attention — watch for this.

Finish by wishing the person well, even if you have tried to persuade them to stay and failed! It does nobody any good to send an employee off with a bitter taste in his or her mouth.

FOLLOW-UP

Decide if action is necessary in the light of any information gained. Implement action.

TERMINATION INTERVIEW CHECKLIST

OBJECTIVE

- To discover a person's real reason for resigning, in order to prevent others from leaving and as feedback on recruitment success

- To secure the employee's goodwill by wishing them well

- Sometimes — to persuade an individual to change their mind

PREPARATION

- check letter of resignation
- study personal file
- chat to workmates/friends
- check room for privacy
- allow plenty of time

SKILLS

- explain the purpose of the interview
- ask open questions
- be friendly, and listen carefully
- finish by wishing well

FOLLOW-UP

Decide if action needs to be taken on any information gained

EFFECTIVE MEETINGS

Most meetings are a waste of time. People often wonder why they are there and find meetings a demoralising experience.

Many vitally important decisions in industry are made during meetings and yet meetings themselves tend to be unproductive, time-wasting and just plain boring. Too many people spend too much time talking about irrelevancies.

In any organisation there is a very good chance that better decisions would be made by half the people in half the time. Democracy in the sense of letting everyone vent their feelings may be philosophically admirable but is commercially suicidal. A strong, well-organised chair can suppress the trivia, elicit the important from those in the know and speed decision-making.

This book therefore aims to set out some clear guidelines for anyone who is involved in chairing meetings or leading discussion groups.

The guidelines are practical and will contribute to making meetings more productive and efficient, whether they are formal committees or *ad hoc* gatherings.

WHAT IS A MEETING?

It is easy to think of meetings only in terms of the large formal variety, but a meeting is any occasion when a group of people come 'together' to share ideas and experiences.

Such meetings differ widely in their size, composition, organisation and purpose, but they all have certain things in common:

- they all exist for a purpose

- they all involve people communicating with one another

- they all have someone in control

It is fundamental to the success of any meeting that the purpose is clear and relevant. Unless the meeting serves a useful purpose, it not only wastes valuable time and effort but it can cause frustration, misunderstanding and can generally demotivate people.

Meetings can become an end in themselves. This is especially true of regular meetings which tend to take place just because they always have done. Regular meetings do have their uses but it is essential that there is some worthwhile business to discuss.

Meetings serve a variety of purposes, but broadly speaking they are concerned with:

- information giving

- information gathering

- persuading

- problem solving

- decision taking

The way a meeting is organised and the role of its leader can vary accordingly.

RESPONSIBILITIES OF THE CHAIR

The leader of any meeting has a variety of responsibilities which include:

- defining the purpose of the meeting

- planning and preparation

- attending regularly

- conducting the meeting efficiently

- controlling the discussion without doing all the talking

- dealing effectively with problem situations and individuals

- ensuring the meeting keeps to time

- making sure the purpose of the meeting is achieved and members know what is expected of them as a result

- liaising with the secretary to ensure that an efficient recording mechanism exists where required

In many instances the secretary of a committee or meeting will take responsibility for organising the date, time and place of the meeting. The secretary may also draw up and circulate the agenda and write and distribute the minutes. For maximum efficiency there needs to be some level of consultation between the meeting leader and the secretary on the agenda and minutes.

The next sections of this book will deal with:

- planning and preparation for the meeting, including drawing up an agenda

- the skills of chairing the meeting

- minutes and any further follow-up action required.

PLANNING AND PREPARATION

A well-planned meeting has a much greater chance of success than one that is called at five minutes' notice and has not been well thought out.

There are three areas where planning and thorough preparation can assist the leader of the meeting:

- define the purpose of the meeting

- planning the content of the meeting — the agenda

- planning the domestic arrangements for the meeting

DEFINING THE PURPOSE OF THE MEETING

There are two questions which need to be answered here:

- what is the purpose of holding this meeting?

- is the purpose going to be best achieved by holding a meeting?

Many meetings are ineffective because the purpose is not clear, not only to the person who has called it but to others attending. This is particularly true of regular monthly meetings, for example. The main purpose of these sometimes seems to be the self perpetuation of the monthly meeting.

It is, therefore, crucial that the person calling the meeting asks the question 'What is the purpose?' before doing anything else. It is sometimes a good idea to write the purpose down in one or two sentences so that it is clear and can be stated at the beginning of the meeting if necessary.

Once the purpose is defined it is worth asking the second question. Sometimes the assumption is automatically made that a meeting is necessary when in fact several telephone calls or a memo would serve as well.

It is certainly true that if the leader cannot clearly state the purpose of the meeting being called, a meeting is not necessary at all.

PLANNING THE CONTENT OF THE MEETING — THE AGENDA

For any meeting to succeed the participants need to have a good idea of what is going to be discussed and why they are there. The most effective way of ensuring this is to distribute an agenda detailing the topics to be discussed, who is to be there, where the meeting is to be held and, if possible, the approximate time the meeting will take.

The agenda should fulfil two basic functions:

- inform the members of the topics to be dealt with, why they are being discussed and what contribution could be prepared beforehand

- act as a structural basis for discussion

The agenda should be as detailed as is necessary and not just a list of headings.

The meeting leader also needs to plan at this stage a rough guide of how the meeting will be conducted. The actual skills of chairing will be important here and are detailed on page 127.

In planning procedure and conduct, however, the leader will need to prepare an introductory statement which should include the purpose of the meeting. It is also a good idea to prepare the opening question which will get the discussion started.

PLANNING THE DOMESTIC ARRANGEMENTS FOR THE MEETING

The leader is responsible for calling the meeting and deciding who is to attend, although in some instances the secretary will carry out this duty, together with organising the room and the time.

Three points are worth mentioning here:

RECORDING THE MEETING

In all cases it is essential that someone is appointed to take notes or minutes. A major cause of unsuccessful meetings is where the meeting leader also tries to take notes. Neither role can be carried out effectively by the same person. Conflicts of interest may arise if the note-taker is also a participating member of the meeting. Ideally, someone who is *au fait* with the subject matter, but not directly involved, is in the best position to take notes.

VISUAL AIDS

Sometimes it is necessary to use visual aids in meetings, especially where short presentations are being made. They should be planned carefully and below are a few hints on their use:

- **Check** any equipment *before* starting to talk. Always be prepared for the worst (spare bulbs, extra leads, etc.).

- **Plan** the use of aids to complement the talk. Do not rely on any visual aid — always be prepared to talk without it if necessary. Don't just use slides as 'verbal printouts'.

- **Limit** the number of visual aids to be used. Too many distract and confuse.

- **Give time** for people to read slides — do not talk and show slides simultaneously — remove slides immediately after use.

- **Talk** to the group, not the slide, screen or board.

- **Keep it simple** — avoid abstract words or over-complicated diagrams or too much material on one slide.

THE MEETING PLACE

The meeting place should be comfortable and convenient and free from noise and interruptions, such as telephone calls and 'through traffic' of other people. Those attending should be seated so they can all see and hear one another. A round table helps this aspect greatly as well as not creating a hierarchical seating arrangement.

CO-OPERATING WITH THE SECRETARY

The meeting leader and the secretary can benefit from having a short get-together before the meeting starts.
The following topics can be usefully discussed:
- **Technical terminology** if the secretary is unfamiliar with any of the terminology to be used, the meeting leader can explain some of the words or terms most likely to arise.

- **Structure of the meeting** to aid the note-taking they can discuss how the meeting will be chaired.

- **Type of minutes needed** they can discuss and decide on the type of minutes needed, i.e. action notes, verbatim record, threads of discussion and decisions etc.

- **Summarising** the secretary can encourage the use of summaries to make the note-taking easier.

- **Clarifying the discussion** the secretary can establish the acceptability of interrupting the meeting for clarification if unsure of what to note down for the minutes.

Co-operation between both parties is essential to the success of meetings and will avoid lengthy drafting and re-drafting of minutes afterwards.

THE SKILLS OF CHAIRING MEETINGS

The leader of a meeting has a number of skills available which will help maintain control of the discussion during meetings. The leader should not do all the talking. One of the responsibilities is to ensure that everyone participates as well as making sure that particular members do not dominate.

The four main skills for achieving this control are:

- **processing the discussion**
- **statements**
- **questions**
- **summaries**

PROCESSING THE DISCUSSION

OPENING THE MEETING

The leader should be ready to welcome the members and should open the meeting in a friendly manner. This will help to create the right climate. Maintaining the climate depends even more on the leader's ability to inspire confidence and command respect. This can be achieved by demonstrating that the leader considers the meeting important, has planned and prepared for it and knows how to run it. Flexibility is required though it may be necessary to adapt the plan to suit the needs of the members.

The meeting should start with an introductory statement summarising what the meeting is for, what is known, what is required and how it is going to be tackled.

CONDUCTING THE MEETING

One problem that can arise, especially when discussing emotive subjects where people have strong views, is separating factual information from opinion. One approach that can help is:

- **Seeking information** – asking members just for this and keeping them to the point

- **Diagnosing** – reaching a clear picture based on the facts and summarising

- **Seeking opinion** – opinion at this stage

- **Evaluating** – fact and opinion together

- **Deciding** – where do we go from here

The leader should be aware of the needs of the group and should draw out silent members and control the talkative or garrulous. The leader should prevent private discussion in splinter groups.

The leader's participation will vary according to the type of meeting, but it should be remembered that maximum participation by the leader means minimum participation by the members.

CONCLUDING THE MEETING

Achievement of the objective is the whole purpose of the meeting. The leader needs to establish and emphasise this achievement and commend individual and group contributions. Even if the result has not been entirely satisfactory, the leader should try and emphasise the positive aspects.

The leader should make a final summary confirming the conclusions of the meeting and stressing action and who is to take it.

STATEMENTS

There are a number of statements that the leader needs to make during a meeting, and they achieve different purposes.

OPENING STATEMENTS

An opening statement is necessary to clarify the purpose and objectives of the meeting and define the terms and scope of the discussion. It is worthwhile having a positive start to give direction to the group.

INFORMATION

The leader may need to feed in statements to provide information where necessary.

CLARIFICATION

Misunderstanding can arise in meetings and a statement of fact can help to clarify these.

QUESTIONS

Questions can be used to make sure there is maximum relevant participation. The following types are particularly useful.

OPENING QUESTIONS

These should:

- be thought-provoking, and engage the attention of the whole group

- be specific, and related to the experience of the whole group

- start with how, where, when, why, what or who, to avoid a 'yes' or 'no' reply

- point the meeting in the right direction

OVERHEAD QUESTIONS

A question addressed to the group as a whole. This has the advantage of not embarrassing individual members who may be unprepared or unable to answer, and engaging the attention of all members, so there is a good chance someone will reply. An overhead question is useful as an opening question, or to refocus irrelevant discussion. For example, *'What remedies for this situation have we found?'*

DIRECT QUESTIONS

A question addressed to a particular individual. This can be used for a variety of purposes: to bring in a person with special knowledge; in dealing with the retiring, talkative and other problem individuals; to help the meeting when flagging, by asking the resourceful or talkative member for an opinion; to speed up the pace of the meeting. For example, *'Mr A, what is your company's redundancy policy?'*

RE-DIRECTED QUESTIONS

To avoid the meeting's moving back and forth between individual members and the leader, statements and questions raised by one member can be passed to another for comment. This can also be used as a link to co-ordinate a number of points and thus ensure continuity of ideas. For example, *'Miss B, how do you think Mr A's policy of avoiding redundancies by not replacing employees who leave would work in your company?'*

RELAY QUESTION

A question put to the leader is relayed to members for reply. This is useful when the leader does not wish to express any views, get involved in an argument or influence the conclusions of the group. For example, *That's a good question. How did the rest of you deal with that problem?*

REVERSE QUESTION

The person posing the question is asked to answer it themselves. This may be used if the person is known to have views which should be expressed, or to encourage that person to think again. For example, *'I know you have considerable experience of that subject: can we hear what you think?'* or *'I was about to ask you the same question — what do you think?'*

SUMMARIES

The use of interim and final summaries is one of the most powerful skills available to the leader.

INTERIM SUMMARIES

These serve to

- indicate the progress or lack of it
- re-focus off-track discussion
- tie-up one point and move on to the next issue
- highlight important points

- guide the minute-taker
- clarify misunderstandings

FINAL SUMMARY

This establishes the group's conclusions, points to action and gives members a sense of what has been achieved.

Both interim and final summaries should be put to the members for their agreement. This practice will also help the minute taker and cut down on unnecessary argument about the accuracy of the minutes.

PROBLEM PEOPLE AND PROBLEM SITUATIONS

Problems can arise in meetings because different individuals have different interests, and also because the situation itself may be problematic in some way.

A few guidelines follow which may help in dealing with these difficult situations:

PROBLEM PEOPLE

Meeting leaders have to deal with group members each of whom has a different character and very often different interests to protect. It is useful to consider several types which leaders most frequently come across and to look at ways of dealing with them.

THE BULLDOG

They are aggressive and always want to win. Sometimes they have not understood the point. They need to be brought round using the other members of the group. If they remain persistent or are looking for a fight it is better not to draw on them. Put them in the 'dead corner' on your left and pretend not to hear them. Keep cool and if they say something constructive then bring them in.

THE HORSE

They are keen and enthusiastic and know what they are doing. They are intelligent but may talk too much. A skilful way of interrupting them is by taking up one of their statements. If they come too much to the fore the others may become jealous. Make it clear that everyone will have a chance of saying their bit.

THE FOX

They are crafty and capable of slipping banana skins in the path of everyone, including you. Red herrings are their speciality. It is best not to tackle them as they always find ways of escape. You should keep your head. It is better to ask the group what they think of their contributions, giving them the opportunity of making fools of themselves.

THE ARTFUL MONKEY OR 'KNOW ALL'

They can be useful too. One can present through them what others should understand. From time to time act as if they were not there. When they interrupt ask them exactly what they mean and let them get out of their depth with the others doing the questioning.

THE HEDGEHOG

Deep down they despise all the others. They have ability but are sceptical of everything new. They think the others ought to know how to extricate themselves the same way they do. They are not inclined to be helpful. You must show them that it would be of benefit if they put their own experience and knowledge to the service of the others. Give them the chance to get their ideas accepted and this will make it possible for them to listen to the ideas of the others. Encourage them to make a worthwhile contribution and thank them when they do.

THE GAZELLE

They are the timid and retiring type. Make them appear important in the eyes of the others. Ask them direct questions which they are sure to be able to answer. Give them encouragement — they may be valuable.

THE FROG OR 'BLABBER-MOUTH'

They talk too much and often off the point. Say to them *'this is interesting, but could we discuss it another time'*, and start questioning someone else.

THE HIPPOPOTAMUS

They are not interested in anything and make no attempt to hide the fact. They are incapable of adopting someone else's ideas. Try to get them to talk about something to do with their own work.

THE GIRAFFE OR 'STIFF NECK'

They watch the others talking and feel superior to them. You should say *'Yes, it is right for your Department, but should not apply here'*. You should treat them with respect and show you are grateful. They are sensitive and easily offended.

PROBLEM SITUATIONS

The meeting leader may have to deal with difficult situations in meetings not least because of the subject matter, including the following:

UNPOPULAR DECISIONS

Leaders may find themselves under attack from individuals or the whole group. They must be prepared to present their case, acknowledging the weaknesses, anticipating the opponent's objections and emphasising the positive aspects. If there are members of the group in support of the case, encourage them to express their views — these may carry more weight than those of the leader.

BAD NEWS

This has to be told sometimes. Try to find a positive side.

LACK OF INTEREST

Recognise that every item on the agenda cannot be of equal interest to everyone. The possible causes of this are:

- the wrong items have been selected
- too many items dealt with, so attention wanes
- case poorly presented so that relevance to members is not clear

Some remedies are:

- direct questions to individuals, e.g. *'How does this affect you?'*

- drop the subject entirely and return to it later, dealing with a more interesting subject in the meantime.

DISCUSSION GOING OFF TRACK

This can be indicative of lack of interest. The group may start talking about other things or asking irrelevant questions. If there is genuine concern over something else which is worrying the group, it is best to deal with it. Otherwise frequent summarising will help to keep the discussion on course.

STATUS DIFFERENCES

It is the leader's responsibility to protect the weaker members of the group. If there are more junior members present, it is often a good idea to ask for their ideas first. They may be unwilling to express a view once more senior members have made their position clear.

STATING YOUR CASE AT A MEETING

The best preparation and planning can be lost if anyone at a meeting finds it particularly difficult to actually state their case coherently. Some people find it particularly difficult to put over their ideas to a group and will remain silent for fear of being ridiculed if they speak.

Effective speakers know exactly what they want to say. They know how they are going to present their argument. Effective speakers have something to say and say it well. In contrast the ineffective speakers are never clear in their own mind as to what they intend saying. As they speak they dart about in verbal confusion, following no set plan and developing no logical argument. In other words they 'waffle'.

Some of these problems can be overcome by following the rules below:

- **Be sure of the facts.** Sum them up briefly and define any terms that need explaining. State the proposition.

- **Face the snags.** Weigh what is against you and anticipate objections. This also acts as a check on the soundness of your reasoning.

- **Prove your case** by selecting and highlighting your best reasons for the proposition. The strength of the argument will depend on the **quality** not the quantity of your reasons.

- **Show practical evidence.** Have instant examples available to support your facts, but be careful not to slant the evidence to suit your case.

- **End** by repeating the proposition.

By following these simple rules and by having thought out your arguments before the meeting, persuading people to your viewpoint will be made simpler.

MINUTES AND FURTHER FOLLOW-UP ACTION

It is essential that minutes are produced but they will vary depending on the type of meeting. Formal committees sometimes require detailed minutes, where informal meetings may only produce an action list of things to be done as a result of the meeting. Whichever is the case it is important that minutes:

- are produced quickly

- are accurate

- are not a verbatim report

- show what action is required and by whom

The leader of a meeting should note the following points which will help the minute taker to produce accurate and concise minutes:

- summarise at the end of each point on the agenda. In most instances this is all that is required in the minutes and a summary will help the minute taker, especially if the material is unfamiliar.

- spend a few minutes before the meeting with the secretary outlining your plan of how the meeting is going to progress. A general structure will assist greatly in note-taking.

- explain any unfamiliar terms or expressions, particularly technical jargon which may be used during the meeting.

- encourage the secretary to interrupt if a point has not been fully understood.

Where follow-up action is required it is important to monitor progress. Giving individuals deadlines for follow-up action is useful. 'As soon as possible' means different things to different people. If precise dates are given during the meeting and recorded in the minutes, monitoring progress is a much more straightforward task.

RAPID READING

This chapter should help you towards a more efficient method of reading and to point out a few bad habits which may be slowing you down. As a result of practising on the lines suggested in this book, you will be able both to increase your speed of reading and improve the quality of your comprehension and retention. It is important to recognise that the right approach to reading is as important as reading 'rapidly'. It is efficiency we should aim at, and not the sort of misconceptions mentioned below.

MISCONCEPTIONS

THE MAGIC WAND THEORY

People often ask the inevitable question: '. . . *quickly, can you tell me what the secret to speed reading is?'* Many people assume that a book or a course on rapid reading will act rather like a fairy godmother's magic wand passing over them . . . that they will automatically become speed readers once they know what the 'gimmick' is. There is no 'secret' formula, there are no 'gimmicks': there is merely a great deal of practising with the right attitude. The reason that results often appear spectacular after a course of personal practice is that most of us read with the wrong approach and develop bad habits as we grow up; once these are eliminated actual speed is obviously increased.

THE 'FASTER-THAN-LIGHT' READER

Another common fallacy is that after learning the techniques and doing some practice, one could easily read the whole of the *Sunday Times* in five minutes during breakfast, or get through the complete works of

Shakespeare on the train going to work. It cannot be done, at least not if you want to take in anything you are reading. No course or book will enable you to achieve these amazing feats, only an act of God will do this!

This chapter contains good practical advice. It will improve reading ability very greatly if:

- you adopt a new attitude to reading

- you adhere to the techniques and suggestions in this chapter

- you practise this new approach regularly.

THE SKILLS OF READING

What are the skills that we have to develop? Let us relate them logically to the reading process itself. On the following page is a diagram outlining the basic reading process.

This may appear to be a very complicated and lengthy procedure, but in fact the mind in reality performs every one of these stages almost simultaneously. Perhaps we have just come up against our second major barrier — that of fearing the limitations of our brain. Apart from the obvious limitations of vocabulary in some cases, intelligence bears no relation to reading ability. The exception to this may be the person of below average intelligence. Provided that one is above average intelligence, then a person with an IQ of 120 is likely to be just as good a reader as the person with an IQ of 180 (maybe even better). Our brains are capable of far more than we imagine, and it is unfortunate that most of us grossly underutilise our minds in everyday life. To read efficiently, we need to use them to their fullest extent, and not underestimate their capabilities.

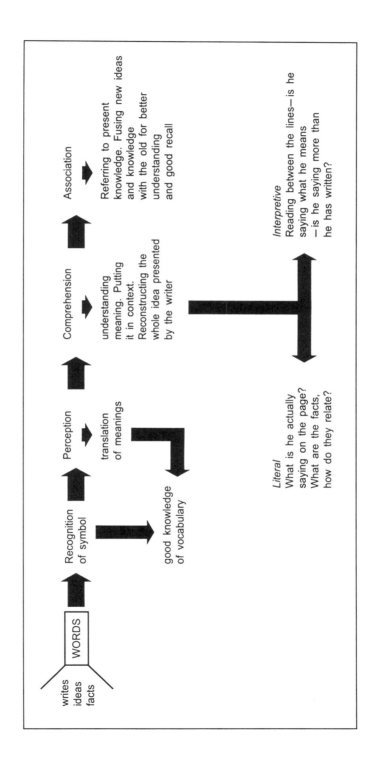

SPEEDING UP

As most of our training in reading finished at the recognition stage, few of us develop independently towards advanced reading and many of us become lazy in our reading habits, so that an average person on average material will read at around 250 words per minute (that is about a foolscap page of longhand writing). This is too slow. The many rapid reading courses that have developed in recent years attempt to help the reader to adopt new habits and develop a much faster style of reading. It must be pointed out, however, that as we get older many of us suffer from recognition problems due to poor eyesight — have your eyes tested regularly.

sophie

HOW FAST DO YOU READ?

It is very difficult to assess reading speed without having any guidelines.

EXERCISE

In order to find out whether you are a fast or slow or average reader, turn to the Pyramid Effect exercise on page 183 and do a reading test before going any further.

The exercise you have just completed also tested comprehension of the material. This is most important because it is one thing to read at 600 words per minute and have a good understanding of a passage, and to read at 600 words per minute and not know the first thing about it. The speed of reading must always be considered in conjunction with the understanding of what has been read. On material of this difficulty an average reader would expect to get between 60 and 70 per cent comprehension with a speed of about 250 words per minute. This may act as a rough guide to your own present ability.

Some people naturally read more quickly than others. This is not related to intelligence or, as far as we know, any other such factor, age, sex (although many men complain that their wives are amazingly fast). It must, therefore, be related to the technique employed in reading.

EYE MOVEMENT

Let us look at the physical factors involved in reading. How do our eyes move? Most people, asked the question, would reply that the eyes move smoothly across the page from left to right along each line and back again, as in the diagram here:

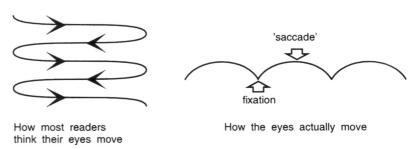

'saccade'

fixation

How most readers
think their eyes move

How the eyes actually move

This is not the case, however. In 1890 a French ophthalmologist called Emile Javal disproved this theory by testing people's eye movements as they read. He discovered that eyes do not move smoothly at all. In fact they 'jump' from one focus to the next. Javal termed the 'jumps' as 'saccades' and the focusses as 'fixations'. From this discovery other interesting points were noticed. A fundamental difference could be traced between the fast and the slow reader by monitoring these eye movements. The same passage was read more efficiently by one reader than the other. The following examples will illustrate the differences noticed.

It should be noticed that there are two major differences here.

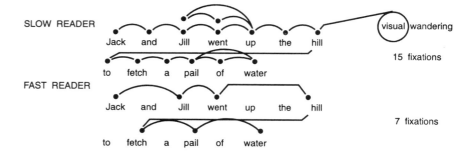

SLOW READER

Jack and Jill went up the hill

visual wandering

to fetch a pail of water

15 fixations

FAST READER

Jack and Jill went up the hill

7 fixations

to fetch a pail of water

- the slow reader fixes on every word

- the slow reader goes back, 'regresses', to re-read certain words, as well as wandering at times

FIXATIONS

So a critical factor in faster reading is the number of fixations.

Obviously, this is not the only problem, for the length of time taken for each fixation is also important. The time taken for each focus can vary between 1/5 second and $1^1/_2$ seconds. Some readers would obviously benefit from attempting to quicken this time to be nearer the 1/5 second minimum. This is perfectly possible for us, as the brain can register as many as five words in 1/100 second. It is a question of accepting that we are merely *recognising* the words in order to interpret them and *not* attempting to pronounce them — this will slow up fixation time *and* prevent us from breaking the 'reading-every-word' habit.

Let us examine what sort of a difference these two points make. Taking the number of fixations alone:

    – the slow reader makes 15 fixations
    – the fast reader makes 7 fixations.

If we assume, for the sake of this argument, that they both have an average fixation time of 1 second, then our slow reader takes 15 seconds and our fast reader takes 7 seconds to read the same material. Magnify this by a whole page and then an entire book and the difference becomes very significant. If it takes the fast reader a week to read a book, it takes our slow reader at least two weeks! In terms of a year's reading of books, this means that one gets through 52 books in a year, while the other will get through only about 25.

Let us look at fixation time next. Again, if we assume that both our slow and our fast reader make 7 fixations, if one fixes for $1^1/_2$ seconds and the other for 1/5 second, then it takes this long:

- the slow reader takes $10^1/_2$ seconds
- the fast reader takes $1^2/_5$ seconds.

Putting both these results together we see that the difference between our slow reader (too many fixations and too long) and our fast reader (a fewer number of shorter fixations) is:

- the slow reader takes 15 fixations of $1^1/_2$ seconds
$= 22^1/_2$ seconds
- the fast reader takes 7 fixations of 1/5 second
$= 1^2/_5$ seconds

Now the difference is considerable!

ACTION TO IMPROVE FIXATION

CUT DOWN THE LENGTH OF EACH FIXATION

This means trying to read faster; not lingering over words; pushing yourself faster all the time. Read another passage and time yourself. It is possible to increase reading speed by 25 per cent by merely willing to do it. Regular tests to monitor speed are very useful to check that speed continues to increase. You should always aim to increase on every exercise. It is only practice that will make a significant improvement here. See appendix 5 for details on how to test yourself at home or at work.

STOP FIXING ON EVERY WORD

This does not mean skipping words — yes, you do *READ* every word, but do not fix on every one. It is very easy to look at one word and see the two words on either side simultaneously. Try it. Fix your eyes on the middle word below and take in the other words without looking at them specifically.

The   cat   sat.

Always try to fix on verbs or nouns. That is, the words that describe what is being done, or what the facts are. Words such as 'and', 'but', 'when' are so common and easy to recognise that they can be taken in along with a fix on a more significant word. This does not mean these words can be omitted or assumed, because missing a 'not' can change the whole meaning of a passage. Consider the sentence below:

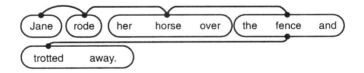

Here the fixations have been made over all the main points made in the sentence. The circles show the limit of each 'eye span' involved, so that when the reader fixes on 'horse', he also takes in 'her' and 'over' in the same eye span.

Notice that there is no fixed 'span'. It would not be sensible, for instance, to decide to fix on every fourth word. The range of each span depends very much on the material being read.

Eye span varies from person to person. Nobody should need to focus on every word, however. Eye span can be increased a small amount by practice. Concentrate on fixing less rather than on trying to stop pronunciation. By doing this and speeding up, you will be forced to stop subvocalising. If you try to concentrate on not pronouncing, however, you will become very confused!

REGRESSION AND VISUAL WANDERING

Often regression (going back over material that has already been read) and visual wandering, can be the result of slow un-motivated reading practices. It is certainly true that if we read too slowly we become bored with what we are reading. This is partly because we have often forgotten what was written at the beginning of the sentence by the time we reach the end. Our eyes are not moving fast enough for our brains. As a result we do not take in the information the first time and are forced to go back and read it again. Regression, then, can be caused by boredom and reading too slowly. Visual wandering is also, obviously, caused by boredom, not having to concentrate sufficiently on the material and therefore drifting off it. Regression, however, can also result from laziness. When we read normally we all know that we can go back and check a word whenever necessary and so our minds become lazy and we are forced to take in the information the first time.

Obviously we must get rid of unnecessary regression. The intelligent reader chooses when to regress. Sometimes it is necessary. For instance, when a new or difficult word is encountered, or where a passage or sentence appears in hindsight to have been of crucial importance, then it is justified. However, what is not justifiable is the habitual going back over words which are quite familiar.

To prevent this it is a good idea to practise reading with a card for a few days to prevent any going back at all. This will break the habit — then the card can be dispensed with.

HOW TO USE THE CARD

Practise this on your reading for the next few days; start now.

NB Your comprehension will suffer initially — persevere, it will be worth it in the end.

Bring down the card at an angle exposing only the text to be read and covering the writing already looked at.

Read *below* the card.

The reader is here

READING FASTER — MENTAL BARRIERS

Just as we have all inherited mental barriers to not reading every word we see, we also developed in childhood the idea that 'reading slowly is reading well'.

This is not true. We have already seen why this idea has developed in education and that there is no need for the stage which so often slows us down, the pronunciation stage. Reading faster often means reading more efficiently. Our minds are forced to concentrate harder if we read faster and do not allow ourselves to regress. There is no time for mental wandering. We also gain a certain impetus of gathering eye rhythm which helps us to read faster and also helps us to put together individual pieces of information into the whole picture which then emerges more clearly. Reading speeds of 1,000 words a minute are possible with comprehension of 70 per cent. This pre-supposes a *wish* to improve speeds and a *belief* that this can and should be done. Again, on a novel or work of art, it is perhaps not necessary or desirable to read quickly. Most of our reading problems boil down to lack of motivation to read faster. Do another exercise now, forcing yourself to read faster. You will find that, as with the regression exercise, your comprehension may suffer on the first few exercises because it will take a while for the mind to adjust to the new situation.

Concentration is a common problem. As we have seen above, this can often be cured by improving reading style. One can also do some practice, if this is a problem, at home every day. Just practise in order to concentrate on some reading for one minute. When you are sure that you are not wandering during this minute then extend it to two minutes and then three and so on. You will be very aware of when you have lost your concentration. Do not extend the time until you are sure of the previous one.

This is a simple but sure way of practising concentration and monitoring your improvement. Remember, concentration varies a lot depending on whether you are interested or not in the passage — use the same type of material for each practice.

Use a pencil or pen to direct your concentration. Many people feel that this is detrimental to reading, but in fact it can help the eyes to focus at the right point and prevent visual wandering. Do not move the head from side to side. The only problem arises when the pencil is moved too slowly, then obviously the reading suffers. It is possible, however, to use the pencil to push speeds faster. Do not try to use a pencil while you are still practising with the card! Practise reading fast, turning pages over quickly — reading the same exercise faster and faster. Try using a metronome for rhythm and speed.

Reading very fast in this way improves speed. Do not worry about comprehension while doing this. It is rather like driving along the motorway at 80 mph. Imagine having your speedometer covered over and being asked to slow down to 30 mph. You would do this, only to discover that you had actually slowed back to only 50 mph. You get used to travelling at a faster speed and then find the slower speeds 'too slow'. It is very similar in reading — speed up to 80 mph and when you go back to reading 'normally' you will find you are reading more quickly!

PHYSICAL PROBLEMS

There are other problems besides those of our own techniques. The ability of the writer and the situation in which we are reading also will have a considerable effect on our efficiency. We can allow for these things to a certain extent and this will be looked at when we consider the right approach to reading.

SUMMARY

The reader's eyes move in 'fixations' and 'saccades'. The major difference between a fast and slow reader is in the nature of the fixations:

- Fix less often

- Fix on groups of words and not single ones

- Cut down fixation time by forcing yourself to read faster.

Remember, often a slow reader is an inefficient reader. Push your speed hard. It will seem to be an effort now, but you will read faster naturally after practice.

THE RIGHT APPROACH

FLEXIBILITY

Let us develop our approach to reading now in a wider field. It is not only necessary to be able to rapid read, but to adapt the style of reading to the circumstances. The essence of good reading is in flexibility. The average reader will read the newspaper at 250 words per minute, a letter from Aunt Mabel at the same speed and a report at work also. Flexibility must be applied in two ways:

- with each piece of material the type of reading to be employed can be decided beforehand — which approach is to be used

- within each piece of material the approach may have to be modified throughout according to changes in the material encountered.

WHAT APPROACH?

In rapid reading terms we talk of reading 'gears'. This is how we divide up the various approaches to reading into categories. These gears can be compared to the gears of a car. In a car, starting off in the right gear and changing gears regularly (being flexible) is very important — and so it is in reading. (Except that we are not restricted to starting in first gear every time.)

THE GEARS

What are the gears? There are four:

STUDY READING

Reading at a speed of up to 200 words per minute — can be as low at 50 words per minute. This is a technique of dealing with material and includes the other gears below. Hence it is the *equivalent* of reading at the above speed — it does not involve actually slowing the reading down to 50 words per minute; the same material is read more than once. Used when material is very difficult or 100 per cent comprehension is required. As with first gear in a car — it is a slow but high-powered gear.

SLOW READING

This is the speed at which most people normally read everything. It ranges from about 200–300 words per minute. This gear is of very little use unless the material becomes a little difficult, as normally this is an inefficient speed. Generally, it is more efficient to read a piece twice very quickly than to read it once at this speed. Word by word, line by line progress. Except, of course, for novels, poems.

RAPID READING

This is your most useful gear. It is a speed of between 300–800 words per minute. It involves reading every word (but not fixing on every one). It is used on material of average difficulty and would dictate a level of 60–70 per cent comprehension. This is sufficient for most everyday reading exercises. Line by line progress reading *groups* of words.

SKIMMING

The fastest gear. Speeds range from about 600 words per minute to 60,000 words per minute. Again, as with studying this is a speed *equivalent* to the above words per minute. With skimming, many of the words are not read at all as in reading. Words are missed out. The comprehension value of this exercise is much less than the other gears. It is most useful, however, for getting an overall idea of a passage, or finding specific information. It can be used most usefully in combination with the other gears.

So far we have looked at the difference between gears 2 and 3, efficient and inefficient reading. We will be examining gears 1 and 4 later.

WHAT FACTORS AFFECT THE STYLE OF READING?

There are three major areas affecting the way in which we should approach our reading, to guide us in our use of gears. As with driving a car, when we begin to learn gear changing we have to think about when it is necessary to use third or fourth gear. However, after a few weeks we are changing gear instinctively. As we approach a hazard we automatically change gear. So it is with reading. Changing speed becomes instinctive eventually, although it must be conscious at first. Compare the diagrams overleaf to see how similar rules apply in both cases.

The three factors which decide when we change gear, and indeed decide what gear we start out in when we read are:

- the nature of the material

- our purpose in reading

- external factors.

Let us consider each of these individually.

THE MATERIAL

Several points need to be taken into consideration here. Difficulty is obviously one of the most apparent concerns for us. This could be related to *difficult concepts* involved or *difficult vocabulary*. (Or bad writing which will be dealt with shortly.) Trying to appreciate difficult ideas or concepts in a passage should involve intense concentration and a combination of reading techniques. Reading through once, even very slowly, is often not enough to appreciate this type of material, but a combination of skimming for the main ideas, the whole idea and then rapid reading to fit each individual factor into the whole concept is the best way to tackle this. Or alternatively a study technique may be applicable for a very difficult piece.

On the other hand, if the problem is that of a *lack of vocabulary* or a poor vocabulary letting the reader down, then an effort can be made to improve this, although while it is still poor, obviously it will be necessary to actually stop and examine each unfamiliar word.

Prior knowledge of the subject matter is always a considerable advantage to the reader. Understanding and memory improve on a passage where some facts are easily recognisable. On material of this kind it is obviously most efficient to read a little faster.

Interest in the subject matter can be a considerable influence. An unmotivated reader is a poor reader. Do not slow down to try to make up for lack of interest. This will merely make the boredom more intense. Speed up and force yourself to concentrate harder, impose a discipline by testing yourself for knowledge of the content afterwards.

Badly written material is something that we can only suffer. The style of the author may be unnecessarily verbose, illogical or too brief to make any sense. The layout of the writing is also of great importance — a poor layout will slow reading down as much as a bad writing style.

PURPOSE

Normally we know *why* we are reading, there is a reason. Making sure that we are aware of this before we begin to read is of prime importance. It helps us to be selective in our reading, but it also gives us a clue as to the style of reading with which it should be tackled. Sometimes we need to know the details of some material thoroughly. This may apply, for instance, to the reading of legislation. If we need *100 per cent comprehension* or need to memorise material, then we need to use a study technique, gear one. If, on the other hand, we want a *good understanding* of something but do not need to remember all the detail (perhaps with the reading of a report) then gear three, rapid reading, would be the most appropriate.

Finally, if only a *vague outline*, a general idea of the main points, is required, then skimming is obviously adequate. This is often useful for reading documents before meetings, or getting the idea of a report before reading it in gear three. Being *selective* in our approach is a very important step towards efficient reading.

OTHER FACTORS

There are obviously other, external, factors that are going to affect our style. We have to allow for these, although we can often do nothing about them.

Environment — the surroundings in which we decide or have to read, have a tremendous influence on us. Noise and constant *interruptions* are obviously fairly high on the list. If we have built up a good concentration level, however, noise around us can be largely eliminated by our minds with practice. It is perfectly possible to cut ourselves off from the rest of the world if our concentration is funnelled down into one opening — our reading. This technique does not, however, get rid of interruptions such as the telephone and visitors. It is therefore necessary to consider whether it might not be a good idea to set aside reading 'periods' during the day when there are likely to be fewer interruptions. Some people, for instance, always read between 8.30 and 9.30 in the morning, because the office is quiet. Try taking lunch at a different time from most others, so that you can work peacefully while they are at lunch, or reading when most people have gone home at night. There is no easy answer.

The reader's state of mind. This is another factor to take into consideration. What time of day is it? Apart from the points mentioned above, we all have our own time clocks. This means that some of us concentrate more easily in the morning, others around midday, some in the afternoon, evening or early hours of the morning.

Keep a diary for a week and note down the best times for working, and see at the end of the set period whether there is any correlation. This will give you a good clue as to when your reading would be most productive.

Relaxation is most important. Have a relaxed but alert mind and body. Having the right approach to reading will help to reduce tension when there is a time limit. Previously, with half an hour before a meeting and a 60-page document un-read in preparation, you may have panicked, started to read but been so worried knowing that you would not finish, that in fact you took in very little at all. Now looking at the problems objectively and putting together all the facts — you want to know as much as you can about the whole document — your restriction is that you only have 30 minutes in which to do it. In these circumstances, skimming in gear four would give the reader a fair knowledge of what the entire document contains. There may also be time then to go back to the odd sections of the document that you feel may be of particular interest and rapid read these for more detail. Using a method like this, far more will be derived from the material than would have been using the 'read-straight-through' method. Relax and deal with the material in the systematic way.

Relaxation is also a *physical* consideration. It is not a coincidence that typists are told to sit up with their backs straight and their feet on the floor, and that yoga advises the same basic position. In both cases the important point — whether sitting in a typist's chair or in the lotus position on the floor — is that the back should be at 90° to the floor. That is because this is the best position for all the senses to be functioning efficiently. The spinal column is straight and the blood circulation and messages from the nervous system can flow freely to the brain.

Holding the reading material directly in front of the eyes is a great help to our reading also. If the eyes are looking straight ahead, they are fully open and alert. If the book is held in the lap or on a desk then there is a greater tendency for the eyelids to close. Anyone who attempts to read lying down in bed will know that this is the best position in which to fall asleep!

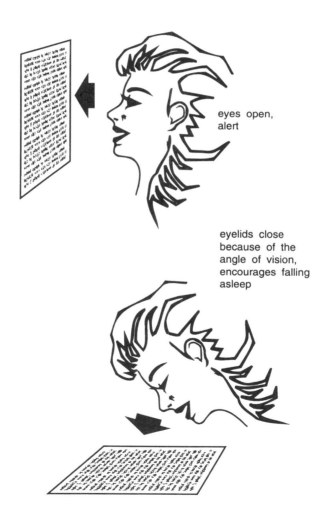

eyes open, alert

eyelids close because of the angle of vision, encourages falling asleep

In order to be truly flexible we have to take all these three areas into account before we start to read, and be able to anticipate necessary changes in our style during the reading itself. The main points can be tabulated as follows:

Purpose	*Material*	*Other*
100% comprehension	• Difficult ideas	• Noise, interruptions
• Memorise material	• Difficult vocabulary	• Time of day
• Good understanding	• Badly written/ laid out	• Relaxation level (time limit)
• General outline	• Prior knowledge	• Emotional barrier
• Particular facts	• Interest	• Personal physical condition

COMBINATION OF GEARS

This choosing the right approach, like choosing the right gear in a car, becomes instinctive after a while. Often it is useful to combine gears to achieve the best results. Skimming can be used most usefully on almost any material as a preview to reading. It can also be used to review the material afterwards. We should not slow down reading speeds. If a preview has been done very rapidly, then the reading should be far faster. It is always more efficient to read something very quickly twice than it is to read it slowly once. Similarly rather than regress during the passage (breaking the rhythm) some readers prefer to mark, mentally, or with a pencil, the points that need to be checked again, and then these points may be reviewed together after the whole passage has been read. Try using these three techniques:

- Preview, then read

- Preview, read, review

- Read, then review

Preview and review are both done by skimming — either before or after reading. Try not to allow this to slow your speed; practise until it is a speedy, efficient process. (See the section on skimming for clues on how to skim — page 175.)

SUMMARY

The right approach involves flexibility of techniques. We must judge both our approach to material as a whole and be prepared to adapt this approach during the reading itself. The three major items that influence this approach are:

- The material

- The purpose in reading

- External factors — in our surroundings
            — within ourselves

A combination of the 'gears' is often the most efficient approach.

UNDERSTANDING AND REMEMBERING

UNDERSTANDING

Having selected the parts that we need to concentrate on, we must achieve maximum understanding. Why is it sometimes easy to understand and at other times almost impossible? Well, a great many factors affect our understanding process. Some of these are:

The material	*The environment*	*The reader*
Difficulty of subject	Interruptions	Lack of interest (or interest)
Difficulty of language	Distractions	Physical fitness — tiredness
Poor layout	Uncomfortable surroundings	Prior knowledge or lack of motivation
Poor style	Too comfortable surroundings	Feelings about the writer
		Own views
		Concentration level

    We have come across these problems in a previous chapter — we can do little about the writing itself except adapt our reading style to allow for it. We can do a little about our environment, but the extent to which it affects our understanding does depend a great deal on our mental state. Therefore, we shall look primarily at the mental state of the reader and its effect on the reader's understanding. First, let us look at the process of understanding itself.

    Information is received by the eyes and transmitted to the brain. Firstly it is divided into what is needed and not needed, then further divided into categories. These categories or 'frames of reference' are shown as squares in the diagram. Similar information is stored together and understanding comes from the comparison of material within the category concerned. We understand by relating new information to similar material that we have already come across.

    Let us look at how this process can be interrupted.

- Lack of interest
  Physical fitness — tiredness   affect concentration
  Motivation

If the concentration is impaired by the factors above then the information will not even be selected, but discarded as not important enough at the select stage.

- Lack of prior knowledge — can mean that the new information will be stored in a 'square' of its own. As there is no other information to relate to, there can be no 'understanding' only a recording of the fact. Here it is important to relate new material to any other material with which there is a connection so that it can be interpreted perhaps through another 'square's' contents.

- Own views and feelings about the writer — the correct meaning is biased by our emotional reactions to the material or writer and therefore the understanding becomes distorted.
  Our reading can be improved by adopting a *critical* approach. This will help the mind to organise material into appropriate categories for interpretation and in the process will involve the mind. Involvement breeds interest and concentration.

RULES FOR BEING CRITICAL

- select consciously material needed and not needed

- question material constantly:
  - how does this relate to what I already know?
  - what is the writer actually saying?
  - is the writer saying what he means?

- do I agree with the writer?
- do the facts support the arguments?

●try to build up a whole picture from the individual points:

- what are the main points?
- is there one important main point?
- what is the writer's objective?

●to move from point to point towards a final conclusion

●to write about a central argument/subject etc.

●summarise at the end in your mind to make sure you have the picture and the main points. If material is a page or more long, summarise material at regular intervals throughout as well as at the end.

EXERCISE

Do not worry about trying to do all the above things at the same time. This may tie you in knots. It is important to work up to it in stages. Gradually all these will be adopted until all are done at once. The mind is very capable of doing this.

- Choose a passage and read slowly while questioning as suggested above

- Using the same passage read through and summarise the content

- Using the same passage, read through building up a picture as you go

- Read through the passage: attempt to do all three.

Use this technique, practising on a different passage each day, at least once a day for the next week. When practising speed reading, forget this practice; eventually you will find that you will be doing this automatically while reading quickly. For the moment, practise them separately.

MEMORY

Memory is, as far as we know, based on several factors:

- Getting the information selected into the frames of reference

- Understanding

- Putting in a strong enough memory 'trace' initially

- Reinforcing information regularly

So memory consists of:

We have already dealt with understanding. It is absolutely necessary to understand before we can remember. Anyone who has attempted to memorise maths at school without understanding what the application is will know how difficult it is.

RETENTION

The facts need to be stored or retained before they can be referred to and used at a later date. Retention is a difficult area to test because we usually only know that we have retained if we can recall. However, if we do not remember it is not necessarily the case that we have failed on our retention — we may merely have failed to recall. But how often do we say 'I know that, but it has just slipped my mind'? We often remember the fact a few days later! So, it is possible to retain and not recall, but many failures in 'memory' occur because not enough trouble is taken in making sure that material is retained.

A 'memory trace' refers to material taken into the mind and the impact it has, as far as strength of memory is concerned. So, we can talk of a weak memory trace making little impact, and strong memory traces having a powerful impact.

Immediate recall is normally only possible from the conscious mind. Information is stored in categories in the conscious for a limited period of time after which the memory trace fades. There is considerable evidence to show that it does not fade 'away' but goes into the subconscious. The information can no longer be immediately recalled at will (except under hypnosis).

The length of time that the information remains in the conscious depends on the original strength of the memory trace. If, for instance, a man daydreams while reading, then there will be a weak memory trace and it will fade very quickly. If he concentrates hard, however, then a strong memory trace which is longer lasting is produced. Unfortunately, even a strong memory trace will fade eventually. For normal purposes a single memory trace may be enough. However, for cases where longer lasting retention is needed, the important factor is reinforcement. It is most important to start reinforcing within the first three minutes after the first reading. Go over the points you want to remember. From then on, reinforcements can be further apart. Gradually build up the strength of the memory trace and you can remember for any length of time — but it is always necessary to remind yourself regularly — if only once a month!

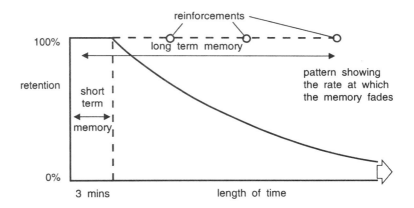

RECALL

Once we have understood and retained the information we need, we can still fail at the recall stage. We know the information is there; what we now need is a foolproof way of being able to fish the information out at will. The two main ways are by using:

- association
- labelling

ASSOCIATION

Not many people are born with 'good' memories; most successful memorisers have a 'system'. The basis of most of these systems is association. There are many ways of using this technique; it is most useful for remembering facts. Of course, many of us use these systems without being aware of it. For instance, how do you remember a telephone number? Look at the number below and decide *how* you are going to memorise it — do not just use a system of rote, this is generally inefficient.

684 9268

WAYS OF REMEMBERING BY ASSOCIATION

- 8 is 2 more than 6 and the last number is 2 less than the first.

Then:

- the last two numbers are the same as the first two in the first set the first number is one more than the last and the only odd number, the second number is 2

Remembering the associations between the numbers helps us to remember the numbers. If you are not mathematically minded, however, try some other versions:

- The 68 bus goes to Grove Road
  The 92 bus goes to Lytham Vale
  The 68 bus goes to Grove Road
  4 is half the last number in the sequence.

Or alternatively:

- Woman with a fat waist   68-92-68
  Remember 4 as above

There are many ways of remembering by association, only a few are shown above. Some methods are easier than others depending on the way your mind works most easily. Your method may not be shown — make one up;

as long as there is a base of association memory will be more effective as a result.

Names of places or people can be dealt with in a similar way:

e.g.　　　　　　　name of person — Duncan Wood — sounds like a Scottish tree

or alternatively,　Duncan is the forename of my uncle and I had a friend at school called (Denise) Wood

Remember the association and nudge your memory about the name!

EXERCISE

Go through the phone book picking out numbers and remembering them using your memory techniques. Go through a newspaper or magazine article and try to remember all the names of people and places and recall them afterwards (forget about speed for this exercise while practising). It is a good idea to read one of the books dealing with memory. This will give you some examples of the many systems developed from the principle of association.

LABELLING

This is a technique which helps us more to remember the context rather than the facts. It is extremely difficult to remember a string of points and it is inefficient to spend the time attempting to. So we can 'label' groups of associated points or happenings. Consider this example:

Remember the following letters and be able to repeat each one in order:

```
M  E  T  H  O  D  I   S  M
I   S  A  N  O  N  C  O  N
F  O  R  M  I   S  T  R  E
L  I   G  I   O  N
```

It would be extremely difficult to read through the letters and remember them by rote. However, we may well make the job easier by grouping and labelling them:

methodism / is / a / non- / conformist / religion

Using this method we do not attempt to remember each letter — we remember six words instead of 33 letters. However, once the words are recalled, we know what letters make up each word, and so we can easily 'work out' the 33 letters.

Labelling works in a similar way. We recognise that a series of facts (or perhaps a paragraph of writing) have a common factor, e.g. they all relate to the legal aspect of the subject. We can, therefore, remember the label 'legal-aspect' and when we come back to produce the facts, the label reminds us of them under its heading.

EXERCISE

Practise going through newspaper articles or a non-fiction book and labelling the main areas of the writing under headings and then remembering these. Recall, using memorised headings.

NB   Be careful to choose an appropriate 'label'. The wrong word can lead the memory off track and floor it entirely!

SUMMARY

In order to understand and remember we must:

- Be selective

- Get understanding by being critical:
  - asking questions
  - building a picture or structure
  - summarising

- Make sure of retention by:
  - putting in a strong memory trace
  - reinforcing the trace regularly

- Make sure of recall by using a system:
  - association
  - labelling

SKIMMING

Skimming can be the busy office worker's most valuable reading tool. When to use it:

- When we want a general outline of the material (scanning/sampling)

- When we only want certain information from a mass of material (locating)

SCANNING AND SAMPLING

The easiest way to practise is on a newspaper.

SCANNING

Do not move the eyes rhythmically in blocks of words across the page as we do in reading. Allow the eyes to wander across the page without regular fixations. The eyes move where they want to, trying to pick out important words. Some people prefer to begin at the bottom of the page and move the eyes upwards — others, to move the eyes diagonally across the page — some move erratically all over the page. The important thing is *not* to have a line by line progress. It does not matter that parts are being missed — we are only after a general impression of the piece. Do it as quickly as you can. Take a newspaper article and get someone to mark how many words are in it. Give yourself a set time limit in which to skim it and begin. (Allow yourself a time limit of about one minute for 600 words.) Stop skimming when the minute is up and try to write down what you remember of the article. Keep practising in this way, gradually increasing the number of words to be covered in one minute.

NB Remember to *concentrate* as you scan, it is very easy to become mesmerised and merely move your eyes across the page without taking in anything.

Scanning: possible pattern
of eye movement
during scanning

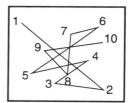

SAMPLING

Sampling is a different technique which achieves a similar result to scanning. When sampling certain parts of the writing are chosen to be 'sampled' to give an outline picture of the whole. For instance, we may choose to read the introductory paragraph, the final paragraph and the first line of each paragraph. In a book we may choose to read the introduction, conclusion and look at all the chapter headings. This is a more structured way of achieving the same result as with scanning — a general outline. Test on a newspaper or magazine as with scanning — but decide before skimming which parts to read. Rapid read the parts to be sampled or, if confident, scan them well.

Sampling: possible pattern

of eye movement

during sampling

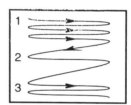

EXAMPLES OF SITUATIONS IN WHICH WE MIGHT CHOOSE TO SCAN OR SAMPLE

- In order to preview material before reading it

- To review material after we have read it

- To refresh our memories of the main points of some material that we are already familiar with or know about

- To find out the bare outlines of a subject if we are pressed for time and cannot read the whole article (e.g. before a meeting)

- To go through very easy or straightforward material

- To get a general outline to increase our general knowledge of a subject without having to spend the time concentrating on it (e.g. trade magazines, newspapers, etc).

LOCATING

We all 'locate' whenever we use a telephone director. If we want to find Mr K Jones we do not start at the beginning and work through until we find him — we calculate by deduction where his name will be. The mental process might be as follows:

- We look for the J's

- We look for 'Jo'

- We look for 'Jon'

- We find the 'Jones'

- We look for 'K' initials

- We find the 'K' Jones'

- We look for the right address

- We find the name

This process of mental deduction is also used for locating material in documents at work. If we require certain information from a document it is time wasting to read it all. We therefore use deduction to discover what we require. Using the index is essential if there is one, and noting the way in which the sections are headed. A good way to practise this method is to use legislation. Take an Act and ask a question about one of its provisions, then calculate where that information can be found before looking for it. Practise at becoming faster each time.

Examples of situations where we might locate:

- To find details of legislation

- To find parts of articles that are relevant to us

- To extract information from a mass of material that we may need to use for a report.

Skimming is very fast — but has a poor capacity for comprehension and retention. It is extremely useful in combination with other methods to aid understanding, but poor on its own unless we need specific information or a general understanding. However, a great deal of material at work often falls into this category and could be 'polished off' very much more quickly using these methods.

SUMMARY

Skimming does not involve reading every word, since when using this technique we purposely miss words and whole passages. It does not involve line by line progress or reading words in blocks.

STUDYING

The word 'studying' has probably conjured up all sorts of memories of schooldays and examinations. In fact, it is a word used to describe a systematic approach to any material that has to be understood fully or memorised. Some material cannot be rapid read — either because it is too difficult in its content, or because more than 70 per cent comprehension is required. The secret to successful studying lies in having a good system of approach. Merely reading the material over three or four times is not sufficient and certainly not very efficient. The most popular study systems use a logical approach to the problem by tackling the material in a way in which the mind will find it most easy to assimilate it. One of the most widely used and popular systems is *SQ3R*. It involves:

S — Survey the material. Skim through it to get the gist — an idea of the 'whole' to fit the parts into.

Q — Question. Decide what questions need to be answered by the material (encouraging the mind to be discriminating).

R — Read the material at whatever speed you are able — normal rapid reading.

R — Recite — that is take notes by going back over the important points. Take *only* key notes to jog the memory later.

R — Revise the notes (not the original material). This is most important — remember the section on long-term memory — it is necessary to revise regularly, particularly at first — in order to strengthen the memory. Revising the original is a waste of time if you have good key notes.

SUMMARY

Studying, or gear one, should be used when the material is difficult; when more than 70 per cent comprehension is needed or when it is necessary to learn the material. The most effective way is to adopt a system of approach which works for you personally.

SUMMARY

Reading well is a question of being flexible and adopting the right approach to material.

- Firstly, get rid of bad habits which will prevent you from reading quickly when the material allows it. Do not worry about pronouncing every word — concentrate on recognising the 'symbol' and read for the *meaning* of the passage. This will allow you to read across the page in 'blocks' of several words taken in by one eye span. (Remember — do not attempt to miss words.) Speed up even more by preventing unnecessary regression. This will enable you to rapid read. Do not worry too much about comprehension while developing this skill — develop speed and then worry about understanding later. Once you are reading quickly enough you will find that you have automatically stopped subvocalising because it is not possible at very high speeds.

● Use the best approach for the purpose and type of material — use the right gears.

● Remember to be critical when reading — question and summarise the material while reading it in order to comprehend properly. Memory involves:
    understanding
    retaining
    recalling
Put in a strong memory trace and use the techniques of association and labelling — trigger and 'key' words to memorise material. *Remember* — a good memory is *developed* using systems, it is not necessary to be born with a photographic memory.

● Skim when a general outline is needed or when specific information needs to be extracted. Use either scanning, sampling or locating but do not read in blocks or make line by line progress. Study where material is difficult or good comprehension or memory is required. Again, use a systematic approach — be efficient.

Once you are reading faster and better — read *more*. Most of us only read what we have to get through at work saying that there is no time for anything apart from this. Often this is an excuse because an inefficient reader gets through a book so slowly that he appears never to get through the whole work! It is important to read as much and as widely as possible to improve reading skills. Why?

Good, fast reading is based on the reader's being able to recognise words (symbols) and interpret them very quickly. It follows that the more familiar the reader is with the words the more easily and quickly he will be able to interpret them. *Any* reading material includes words and so anything will do — although the more widely you read, the less often you will come across an unfamiliar symbol.

The more you read, the more you will want to read, the more interesting different subjects become. Those of you who are sceptical — try it and practise your reading in the process.

READING EXERCISES

Test your starting speed on the following exercises. Use a watch with a second hand. Check time of starting and begin to read. Check finishing time. Write down in minutes and seconds the length of time taken to read the passage.

- answer the test questions
- look up the answers on page 188 and mark the result.

Start now . . .

THE PYRAMID EFFECT

The pyramids on the west bank of the Nile were built by the pharaohs as royal tombs and date from about 3000 BC. The most celebrated are those at Giza, built during the fourth dynasty, of which the largest is the one that housed the pharaoh Khufu, better known as Cheops. This is now called the Great Pyramid. Some years ago it was visited by a Frenchman named Bovis, who took refuge from the midday sun in the pharaoh's chamber, which is situated in the centre of the pyramid, exactly one third of the way up from the base. He found it unusually humid there, but what really surprised him were the garbage cans that contained, among the usual tourist litter, the bodies of a cat and some small desert animals that had wandered into the pyramid and died there. Despite the humidity, none of them had decayed but just dried out like mummies. He began to wonder whether the pharoahs had really been so carefully embalmed by their subjects after all, or whether there was something about the pyramids themselves that preserved bodies in a mummified condition.

Bovis made an accurate model of the Cheops pyramid and placed it, like the original, with the base lines facing precisely north–south and east–west. Inside the model, one third of the way up, he put a dead cat. It became mummified, and he concluded that the pyramid promoted rapid dehydration. Reports of this discovery attracted the attention of Karel Drbal, a radio engineer in Prague, who repeated the experiment with several dead animals and concluded, 'There is a relation between the shape of the space inside the pyramid and the physical, chemical, and biological processes going on inside that space. By using suitable forms and shapes, we should be able to make processes occur faster or delay them.'

Drbal remembered an old superstition which claimed that a razor left in the light of the moon became blunted. He tried putting one under his pyramid, but nothing happened, so he went on shaving with it until it was blunt, and then put it back in the pyramid. It became sharp again. Getting a good razor blade is still difficult in many Eastern European countries, so Drbal tried to patent and market his discovery. The patent office in Prague refused to consider it until their chief scientist had tried building a model himself and found that it worked. So the Cheops Pyramid Razor Blade Sharpener was registered in 1959 under the Czechoslovakian Republic Patent No. 91304, and a factory soon began to turn out miniature cardboard pyramids. Today they make them in styrofoam.

There is a fascinating postscript to this pyramid story. In 1968 a team of scientists from the United States and from Ein Shams University in Cairo began a million-dollar project to X-ray the pyramid of Chephren, successor to Cheops. They hoped to find new vaults hidden in the six million tons of stone by placing detectors in a chamber at its base and measuring the amount of cosmic-ray penetration, the theory being that more rays would come through hollow areas. The recorders ran twenty-four hours a day for more than a year until, in early 1969, the latest, IBM 1130, computer was delivered to the university for analysis of the tapes. Six months later the scientists had to admit defeat: the pyramid made no sense at all. Tapes recorded with the same equipment from the same point on successive days showed totally different cosmic-ray patterns. The leader of the project, Amr Gohed, in an interview afterward said, 'This is scientifically impossible. Call it what you will — occultism, the curse of the pharoahs, sorcery, or magic, there is some force that defies the laws of science at work in the pyramid.'

(543 words)

QUESTIONS

1 What was it about the animals that had wandered into the Great Pyramid that caught the Frenchman Bovis' attention?
2 Describe the experiment Bovis did to test his theory about the pyramid.
3 Describe Drbal's experiments with razors.
4 Describe the reaction of the Czechoslovakian Patent Office to Drbal's patent application.
5 What are Drbal's pyramids made of today?
6 In what direction must a test pyramid be orientated?
7 From where did the team of scientists come who did X-ray studies of the pyramid of Chephren?
8 What did their studies reveal?
9 Where is the most celebrated pyramid?
10 Describe conditions inside the Great Pyramid.

Answers on page 188.

Now, you should have a time written down and a mark out of ten for comprehension of the passage.

Change the time into words per minute — look up the table on page 192. Look down the left-hand column for your time and across the top line for the number of words in the passage. Read across from the left and down from the top. The figure where they meet is your words per minute score.

EXAMPLE:

If it had taken you 3 minutes 5 seconds, look down the left-hand column for 3 min 5 sec and across the top for the nearest number to 543 (number of words in the passage). This gives you a score of 178 words per minute.

Now change your comprehension score into a percentage (multiply by 10) so that 6 out of 10 = 60 per cent.

you now have two scores — words per minute (speed)
— comprehension (percentage)

Keep a record of these, they represent your present speed and comprehension.

KRAKATAU'S TURBULENT CHILD ECHOES CATACLYSM

The Child of Krakatau is growing restive. For the past two weeks, the island volcano has been trembling in the manner of its infamous parent, spewing columns of fire and ash and sending shock waves through the Sunda Strait between Java and Sumatra.

Stepping onto this nightmare landscape of black ash and lava, one is reminded uncomfortably of the cataclysmic explosion that shook the world on August 26, 1883, when Krakatau erupted with the biggest bang in recorded history.

More than 36,000 people died when *tsunamis* (tidal waves) up to 135 ft high swept through the strait at 350 mph and devastated hundreds of coastal villages and towns. The waves were registered in the English Channel, and a giant dust cloud circling the earth created optical illusions and altered the climate of the northern hemisphere for several years.

Sudanese natives blamed the Dutch colonial authorities for failing to offer blood sacrifices to volcano spirits and sea ghosts prowling the area.

From its *caldera* (collapsed crater) 200 metres beneath the sea, Krakatau gave birth to four islands early this

century, but only one survived the pounding surf. Anak
(child of) Krakatau, which emerged in 1930, is now some
600 ft high and growing steadily with the violence of its
progenitor.

An intermittent series of eruptions died down in 1981,
allowing it to become a tourist attraction, but it began
stirring from its slumber again late last month. During
such periods of activity, Indonesian officials urge visitors
to view events from the safety of their hotels on the coast
of west Java, 30 miles away.

This sensible advice is occasionally ignored by small
groups of the brave or foolhardy who charter fishing boats
for 10-hour round-trips from Dr Axel Ridder, manager of
the Carita Krakatau Beach Hotel. Dr Ridder, an erstwhile
West German government employee, doctor of philosophy
and raconteur, likes to shock his clients by informing them
they have an 80 per cent chance of coming back.

'They are totally crazy, *ja!*' he observes cheerfully.
'The professors say you can't predict anything, but we
promise to give them certificates and they go away.'
Dr Ridder hasn't lost anyone yet, but there have been
mishaps. In 1986, two American women were reduced
to living on rainwater and toothpaste when the engine of
their boat failed, and they drifted for three weeks.

A few years earlier, Dr Ridder was standing on
an outer ridge of the volcano when it erupted without
warning. 'You saw everywhere fire-balls, and boulders
were falling all around me. I couldn't take photographs
because my hands were shaking so, and I started to run. I
should be dead already.'

Local experts are not unduly concerned by the
volcano's adolescent tantrums, believing it to be a safe
distance from inhabited regions. But that's what the Dutch
colonial authorities thought in 1883.

(465 words)

QUESTIONS

1 What is the name of the volcano featured in the article?
2 What and when was 'the biggest bang in recorded history?'
3 Name at least one worldwide effect of this biggest bang.
4 In what way does tour operator Dr Ridder shock his clients?
5 What is a tsunami? A caldera?
6 What did the American women adrift at sea eat?
7 How many tourists have been killed on the island this year?
8 On what did the Sudanese natives blame the eruption?
9 What one word is used to sum up Krakatau's child?
10 What overall impression have you gained of volcanic activity in the area?

Answers on page 189.

Note the time taken and your mark out of ten for comprehension. Calculate the words per minute from the table on page 192 and change the mark out of ten into a percentage.

ANSWERS TO READING TESTS

THE PYRAMID EFFECT

1 They had not decayed but were mummified.
2 He made a scale model of the pyramid and placed a dead cat inside, one third of the way up. It became mummified.

3 A sharp razor placed one third of the way up inside a model pyramid did not become dull, but a dull razor placed there became sharp again.
4 They refused his application until their Chief Scientist tried it himself and found it worked. They then granted him a patent.
5 Styrofoam.
6 With base lines facing magnetic north–south and east–west.
7 From the United States and Egypt.
8 The data made no sense at all. 'There is some force that defies the laws of science at work in the pyramid.'
9 Giza.
10 The inside of the Great Pyramid was unusually humid.

KRAKATAU'S TURBULENT CHILD ECHOES CATACLYSM

1 Anak Krakatau
2 Krakatau eruption, 1883
3 Air pollution, waves, climate
4 80 per cent chance of returning
5 Tidal wave, collapsed crater
6 Toothpaste
7 None
8 They blamed the Dutch authorities for failing to offer sacrifices to the volcano and the sea.
9 Turbulent
10 Very active; on-going; brings tourists to the area; at a safe distance from inhabited regions

TESTING YOURSELF

Practise your reading whenever you can. Any piece of writing will do. However, try to choose material of similar difficulty so that your graph will represent a real increase. A harder text will obviously cause you to score lower, and vice versa. It is best to:

- choose a book — and work through that; OR

- always test yourself on the same newspaper

- read a passage, time yourself and record the time

- count the number of words in the passage after you have read it

- work out the two scores — words per minute and comprehension

Test yourself at least once a day; the more you practise the better you will become.

READING SPEED CONVERSION TABLE

Time Taken	400	500	600	700	800	900	1000	1100	1200	1300	1400	1500	1600	Time Taken
0.30	800	1000	1200	1400	1600	1800	2000	2200	2400	2600	2800	3000	3200	0.30
0.35	685	857	1030	1200	1370	1560	1734	1884	2055	2230	2400	2562	2740	0.35
0.40	600	750	900	1050	1200	1360	1510	1648	1800	1960	2100	2250	2400	0.40
0.45	533	668	800	934	1066	1200	1334	1456	1599	1740	1860	2004	2132	0.45
0.50	480	600	720	840	960	1090	1206	1314	1440	1560	1680	1800	1920	0.50
0.55	436	545	660	764	872	988	1096	1207	1308	1420	1520	1638	1744	0.55
1.00	**400**	**500**	**600**	**700**	**800**	**900**	**1000**	**1100**	**1200**	**1300**	**1400**	**1500**	**1600**	**1.00**
1.05	369	461	558	646	746	840	934	1021	1107	1200	1292	1383	1492	1.05
1.10	343	427	525	600	693	780	867	942	1029	1120	1200	1281	1386	1.10
1.15	320	401	483	560	640	720	800	883	960	1040	1120	1203	1280	1.15
1.20	300	375	450	525	604	680	755	824	900	980	1050	1125	1208	1.20
1.25	282	354	425	494	569	640	711	776	846	920	988	1062	1138	1.25
1.30	267	334	400	467	534	600	667	728	800	870	930	1002	1068	1.30
1.35	250	317	380	442	509	573	635	694	750	820	884	951	1018	1.35
1.40	240	300	360	420	483	545	603	660	720	780	840	900	966	1.40
1.45	228	286	344	400	457	517	571	630	684	740	800	858	914	1.45
1.50	218	273	328	382	436	494	548	600	655	710	760	819	872	1.50
1.55	209	261	314	365	419	472	524	575	627	680	730	783	838	1.55
2.00	**200**	**250**	**300**	**350**	**400**	**450**	**500**	**550**	**600**	**650**	**700**	**750**	**800**	**2.00**
2.05	192	240	288	336	384	431	481	528	577	625	675	719	768	2.05
2.10	184	231	276	323	368	413	462	506	554	600	650	693	736	2.10
2.15	177	223	267	311	355	396	445	489	534	580	625	669	710	2.15
2.20	171	215	258	300	342	380	428	472	514	560	600	645	684	2.20
2.25	165	208	249	290	331	370	414	456	497	540	580	622	662	2.25
2.30	160	200	240	280	320	360	400	440	480	520	560	600	640	2.30
2.35	155	194	232	271	310	349	387	426	465	505	545	583	620	2.35
2.40	150	188	225	262	300	339	374	412	450	490	530	564	600	2.40
2.45	146	181	217	255	293	329	363	398	437	475	513	543	586	2.45
2.50	143	174	209	247	286	319	352	384	424	460	495	522	572	2.50
2.55	138	170	204	240	276	309	342	376	412	447	480	511	552	2.55

READING SPEED CONVERSION TABLE

Time Taken	400	500	600	700	800	900	1000	1100	1200	1300	1400	1500	1600	Time Taken
3.00	**133**	**167**	**200**	**233**	**266**	**300**	**333**	**368**	**400**	**435**	**465**	**501**	**532**	**3.00**
3.10	126	158	190	221	253	285	316	348	379	410	440	474	506	3.10
3.20	120	150	180	210	240	269	300	330	360	390	420	450	480	3.20
3.30	114	143	171	200	229	258	286	314	343	370	400	429	458	3.30
3.40	109	137	164	191	219	247	272	300	327	355	380	411	436	3.40
3.50	104	131	157	182	209	236	260	288	313	340	365	393	418	3.50
4.00	**100**	**125**	**150**	**175**	**200**	**225**	**250**	**275**	**300**	**325**	**350**	**375**	**400**	**4.00**
4.10		119	145	166	191	214	240	263	287	310	335	357	382	4.10
4.20		113	136	157	182	203	230	251	274	295	320	339	364	4.20
4.30		110	133	153	177	198	222	244	267	290	312	334	355	4.30
4.40		107	129	150	171	190	214	236	257	280	300	322	342	4.40
4.50		104	124	145	165	185	207	228	248	270	290	311	331	4.50
5.00	**80**	**100**	**120**	**140**	**160**	**180**	**200**	**220**	**240**	**260**	**280**	**300**	**320**	**5.00**
5.30			108	127	146	164	181	189	218	237	256	271	293	5.30
6.00			100	116	133	150	166	184	200	217	232	250	266	6.00
6.30				108	124	139	155	165	185	201	216	232	248	6.30
7.00				100	114	129	143	157	171	185	200	214	229	7.00
7.30					107	120	134	142	160	174	187	200	214	7.30
8.00					100	112	125	137	150	162	175	187	200	8.00
8.30						106	118	129	141	153	165	177	188	8.30
9.00						100	111	122	133	144	155	166	177	9.00
9.30							105	116	127	137	147	158	168	9.30
10.00							100	110	120	130	140	150	160	10.00
11.00								100	109	118	128	135	146	11.00
12.00									100	108	116	125	133	12.00
13.00										100	108	116	124	13.00
14.00											100	107	114	14.00

DICTATION
TECHNIQUES

In most organisations we have a choice when we want
our letters, reports, memos, etc, produced in the typed
form. We can write by hand and send it for copy typing,
we can dictate face to face to a secretary or shorthand
typist and, with today's modern technology, we can
dictate directly over the shoulder of the secretary or word
processor operator and see immediately what we have said
on the VDU screen, or input the information direct onto
our own p.c.s.

Therefore, with so many alternatives, why should
we even bother to consider dictating on tape? It is now
recognised that the dictation machine saves time for both
the originator and the secretary/typist and hence is more
effective. You can dictate when it is convenient for you,
and the secretary/typist can transcribe the tapes at his or
her convenience.

Audio dictation is a skill which can easily be acquired
by following a simple set of rules and ensuring a complete
understanding of the audio system being used. You may
be using a simple hand–held pocket machine; a desk–top
model; or your company may have a centralised system
where authors gain access via the telephone system.
Whichever you use, the same rules apply.

The golden rule — put yourself in the shoes of the
secretary or typist!

Perhaps you have never even thought about this before
or wonder now why you should bother. Perfect audio
dictation requires the skills of two people: one who
originates the work and one who transcribes it. Both need
to understand the other's role and requirements before
they can become the perfect team. Why not discuss this
book with whoever transcribes your tapes after you have
finished reading it?

ADVANTAGES OF USING AUDIO

- saves time and money — whilst you dictate the secretary can do other work

- overcomes bad handwriting problems

- workload can be shared out — i.e. a lengthy draft split on to three tapes can be typed by three people

- cuts out 'waffle' — audio dictation means more planning

- provides additional skills for you and your secretary/typist

- cuts out panic when you want that urgent work at 5 pm — whilst page 1 is being transcribed from tape you can dictate page 2 on tape 2, etc., increasing productivity for both parties and eliminating waiting time

- the machine can be used for leaving messages for your secretary — saves time in writing notes which might get lost

- the machine can be used for making notes and reminders for yourself after a meeting or visit whilst your thoughts are still fresh

The following chapters outline the problems that are sometimes encountered and the ways of overcoming them, the importance of understanding the machines and the rules to be followed to become the perfect dictator.

PROBLEMS

What are the problems frequently experienced by dictators and secretary/typists?

DICTATORS

- speaking their thoughts out loud in open plan offices which some find embarrassing

- distractions from background noises

- not being able to see what you have said (it has 'disappeared' into the machine)

- losing track of what you have said

- getting to grips with the machine

- voice not clear on tape

- accents not familiar to typist

- frustration with secretary/typist when work that is returned bears little resemblance to what was wanted

- remembering the instructions to the secretary/typist

COMMENTS FROM DICTATORS:

'*How* ow *could she type "crawling up the wall"? I distinctly said "calling on you all".'*

'*They type what they think they hear, whether it makes sense or not.*'

'*My secretary said I mumbled, so next time I shouted — now he says the mumbling is louder.*'

'*I thought she would like the background music!*'

'*I don't understand it — I know I dictated a full tape but you say there is nothing on there.*'

*'I wanted the name R Smith so I dictated R for
Roger Smith. Why did the typist type Arthur Roger Smith
then?'*

SECRETARY/TYPIST

- lack of knowledge or interest in dictated subject
- hearing content for the first time
- distractions from own background noise
- inferior quality of tapes
- personal animosity (bad dictator)
- temporary staff
- insufficient information sent with tape
- lack of instructions from dictator — meaning guesswork
- too many instructions from dictator.

COMMENTS FROM TYPISTS:

'His voice is so flat and boring I nearly fall asleep.'*

*'I never get any punctuation at all and then when I do my best,
it's wrong. I'm not a mind-reader.'*

*'My boss has overdosed on instructions — for example he says
full stop — new sentence — initial capital. For goodness sake,
I know that a new sentence comes after a full stop and that
all new sentences begin with an initial capital letter — I'm
not thick.'*

*'I think she has one tape which she has been using for ever. It's
old and scratchy and you can hardly type from it. I also have to*

keep reminding her about the batteries — last week she sounded like Minnie Mouse.'

'He tries to be too clever and dictates very complicated things. I wish he would draw it out on paper and send it with the tape — it would save time for both of us.'

'Why must they give their instructions after we have typed the words. I'm sure they think we play the tape through first and then type it.'

'Most dictators should try typing from tapes and then they would understand why we complain.'

'It's great when you get a good tape — you can type straight through — it makes you feel good.'

THE MACHINE

Whatever machine you use the principles of use are the same.

The machines will:

- run the tape forward

- run the tape back

- stop the tape (when you need time to think or wait for background noise to clear)

- record your words

- erase incorrect words when you record over them

- fast forward the tape (to return to the blank tape after listening or making corrections).

All machines have a manufacturer's instruction booklet or if your company has a centralised system you may already have received personal instruction on the correct use.

The sooner you become very familiar with all the controls on your machine the more time you will have to concentrate on what you want to say and how you want to say it.

Don't panic — you are the master not the machine!

If necessary practise using all controls of the machine by dictating passages from this book. Play back, make corrections, continue recording and keep listening to your dictation. Before long you will find you are using the controls without thinking.

No-one expects you to be perfect from the start — you may be too slow and give too many instructions. The key is to get the balance right and you can only do this by getting regular feedback from whoever transcribes your tapes. Listen to what they have to say.

Note: for users of handheld pocket machines:

- make sure that the red record light is on before you speak — the red light is an indication that you are in record mode. This is very important after you have played the tape back to listen or make corrections

- regularly check quality of batteries and tapes (ask the secretary/typist to throw away poor tapes).

Tapes will last twice as long if you alternate use of both sides

●switch off machine after use (on side of machine). Failure to do this could mean the machine being knocked on accidentally erasing any work on the tape and running down the batteries

●keep in box or pouch provided.

PLANNING AND PREPARATION

Before we switch the machine on it is essential that we consider a number of things:

●where to dictate

●order of work

●priority of work

●deciding what you want to say

●voice presentation

WHERE TO DICTATE

In many cases this will be beyond our control. Today's open plan offices and shortage of space often means that we are sitting very close to our colleagues who could also be dictating, discussing or making phone calls. Others may have their own offices, work from home or stay in hotels whilst working.

Wherever you sit, make sure you are comfortable, that you have the relevant papers handy and try to eliminate as much background noise as possible.

The everyday background noises that we accept in our working lives, i.e. telephones ringing, people shouting, slamming doors, whistling, traffic and music tend to get magnified on tape and can be very confusing to the secretary/typist who is transcribing the tape.

Golden rule — once you realise there is excess background noise stop the tape — shouting through it will only distort your voice and deafen the listener.

ORDER OF WORK

Decide on the priority of your work — what needs to be typed first? If necessary make a list in case you get interrupted.

Are there any files or previous correspondence you need to refer to whilst dictating? 'Flag' these files so that you can turn to these pages quickly.

It is not necessary to fill up a tape completely before you hand it over for transcription. Many secretaries/typists find full tapes demoralising, and remember that once you have dictated four items these can be transcribed whilst you are dictating the next four. Make the system as time saving as possible. This also gives you a natural break — constantly dictating could lead to your speaking too fast, or the voice taking on a monotonous tone.

In centralised audio centres, where tapes are accessed through the telephone system, users are often asked to dictate one item at a time, therefore spreading the work over a number of tapes. This means that the allocation of work is easier and gives other users a chance to access the system. It will also free your own telephone line for incoming calls.

PRIORITY WORK

If you decide that you have a piece of work that is a priority then use a separate tape. It is advisable to keep a number of tapes suitably marked for priority work, i.e. mark with a red dot or use a highlighter pen. In this way the secretary/typist can identify it immediately.

There may be occasions when you realise after submitting a routine tape that one of the items has become a priority. This problem can be overcome by marking the index slip that accompanies the tape. An example is shown here:

Name J. Benn   Date 2 October

1.	2.	3.	4.	5.
Letter to P. Smith	Memo to all Staff	PRIORITY Draft report on salaries	Letter ICAT	

Side A

If you use a centralised audio centre it will be necessary to notify them prior to your dictation, if work is urgent, in order that the tape can be traced immediately.

Golden rule — never use the tape to tell the secretary/typist that a piece of work is urgent or wanted by a certain time.

DECIDING WHAT YOU WANT TO SAY

Put the brain into gear before you put your machine into action!

- plan what you want to say before you start (cuts out the 'thought' noises on the tape); make notes to help you

- make a skeleton of points using key words to prompt you

- decide on structure of paragraphs, tabs, layout, etc. See the picture in your mind so that you can describe it to the typist

- keep sentences short — if using long sentences you will need to playback more often to ensure they are clear

- decide what you can send to the secretary/typist to save you dictating, i.e. previous correspondence containing names, addresses, product names, etc

- are there any standard letters, paragraphs, etc., held on the word processor?

- keep your index slip or typing requisition forms to hand. Complete these as you go along and spread your work over a number of tapes

You will not be perfect on your first tape. You may need to start by making full notes in longhand and dictating into the machine. As you become more confident in this skill and the use of the machine becomes more familiar you can then go on to dictation from key words and short notes.

VOICE PRESENTATION

In order that the secretary/typist can hear and understand it is important that we speak clearly. It will often be necessary to enunciate especially when using words that sound alike but have a different meaning. When dictating do:

- keep the machine, microphone or telephone handset at an even distance from the mouth

- speak in a natural voice at slightly slower than normal speech rate

- speak with feeling and emphasis but this does not mean raising and lowering the volume of the voice

- play back your own tape during recording and listen to yourself

- ask your secretary/typist if your tapes are clear.

When dictating, don't

- mumble

- speak too fast — the secretary/typist is not likely to hear small words such as 'if', 'not', etc., or will miss ending of words or plurals

- speak too slowly — this is frustrating for a secretary/typist with the audio skills of speed and rhythm of transcription

- think aloud — all those 'ums' and 'ahs' made whilst thinking can sound like 'a' or 'are' during transcription

- eat, smoke or drink whilst dictating

- shout or whisper.

DICTATING

Ensure that you always start at the beginning of the tape and rewind if necessary.

From now on you will need to remember that the secretary/typist can only type what they hear you say. They do not know what you are going to say. Imagine that they are blind and you have to paint the picture with your instructions.

The amount and depth of instructions required will depend on who is going to do the typing and how familiar they are with your work. The PA or secretary will be very experienced and have little difficulty; an audio typist/typing pool or temp may rely heavily on guidance.

Remember — when typing from longhand the secretary/typist can read ahead, and with shorthand dictation they will have heard it before — *but* with audio they hear and type in blocks.

The key is to get the balance right when giving instructions — treat the person who types your tapes like a human being — help where necessary — but do not treat him or her like a fool.

Golden rule — find out from your secretary/typist what he or she needs to know from you to do the job properly and eventually save time and frustration for you both.

Discussion on the following instructions could be the starting point:

INSTRUCTIONS AT THE START OF THE TAPE

- greeting — good morning, afternoon, hello — use name of the secretary/typist if you know it — or say *'Typist'*

- say who you are, date and where you can be contacted if necessary, i.e. extension number

- number of items on tape (will be possible if you have planned).

If you are a manager whose secretary sometimes signs post in your absence, it is helpful to notify him or her at the start of the tape if he or she is to do so on this occasion. Many secretaries like to use the clause — 'Dictated by Mr ?? and signed in his absence' —at the end of the letters.

INSTRUCTIONS AT THE START, DURING AND AT THE END OF EACH ITEM

START

- what it is — letter/memo/report/minutes

- if it is confidential, private, etc

- size — long or short — if your company uses both A4, A5, etc

- draft or final copy

- any particular layouts or precedents to be followed

- use of any glossaries stored on word processor

- any files or previous correspondence attached which may contain extracts to be included in typing

- any technical words — these should be spelt *once* only

- any abbreviations or jargon — spelt out

- **extra copies required**

Many companies have designed typing requisition slips to accompany tapes which should be filled in by the originator to overcome the necessity of dictating some of the above. You may need to check what is used in your company.

DURING

House style — you will need to ascertain from the secretary/typist in what order they require certain information, i.e.

- your reference

- their reference

- addressee

or

- addressee

- our reference

- their reference

The order will depend on the house style in use and is also important if letters, memos, etc., have been glossaried on word processors.

Punctuation — the secretary typist has no sense of the structure of a sentence when it begins and cannot punctuate as he or she goes along. Therefore, all punctuation is your responsibility.

.	stop or full stop (*not* 'period')
,	comma
;	semi-colon
:	colon
:–	colon dash
"" or ''	quotation marks or quote
()	brackets or open brackets
x - x	x hyphen x
x – x	x dash x

Paragraphs — always state when a new paragraph is required.

> Note: if you wish to include a paragraph which is inset like this one, ask for an *inset* paragraph.

Remember — when you want to return to a normal paragraph ask for 'new paragraph — back to the main margin'.

Sentences — indicate the end of a sentence by using a full stop. There is no need *ever* to ask for a 'new sentence'.

Tabulation — because of the complexity of the instructions which are needed to explain your requirements for tabulation work, it often saves time if you send hand-written tabulation with the tape. This can be used for checking against after typing.

However, should you decide to dictate these you will need to remember that the dictation must be line by line across the page and not down the columns.

Spelling — this is perhaps the hardest part — sorting out what we need to spell out and when we need to spell it.

We said earlier that it is best to warn the secretary/typist, at the beginning of the item, of any technical words or jargon that you know you will be using, and spell them out.

There will also be occasions when you need to clarify words where the secretary/typist is likely to make a mistake i.e. names, place names, unusual words, product names, for example Davis/Davies, Ezee-Kleen Company.

When and how to do it — say the word first followed by the instruction *'Typist, I spell'* and then clarify:

> e.g. Mendacity — dictate *'mendacity — Typist, I spell m.e.n.d.a.c.i.t.y.'*

Remember — it is not necessary to repeat spelling of words in the same piece of dictation.

Phonetic alphabet — when you spell letter by letter and use letters in postcodes and references it is important to remember that there are letters in the alphabet which sound very similar, i.e. s/f; m/n; t/d; p/b; i/y.

To make sure the secretary/typist knows exactly what you want you must use a 'phonetic alphabet'. Your own simple version would do, e.g. M for Mother, D for Dog, etc.

Do not go overboard — the phonetic alphabet is only used for letters which could cause doubt and is not used for every letter of the alphabet!

Numbers — should these be typed as words or figures? Again it might be necessary for you to check if there is company policy here. A number of companies have the following guidelines for the use of numbers in typed text:

> Numbers under 10 — type in words
> Numbers over 10 — type in figures

Exceptions usually include: at the beginning of
sentences or paragraphs
- in dates
- in house numbers
- sums of money preceded by £ sign

To dictate figures use the instruction *'Typist please —
figures'* and then dictate figures digit by digit:

e.g. 135 — dictate — *'figures one three five'*
not *'figures — one hundred and thirty five'*
70% — dictate — *'figures seven zero per cent sign'*
not *'figures — seventy per cent'*.
(Take care when dictating 13 or 30, 14 or 40, 15 or
50, etc. as it is hard to distinguish them and they
should always be clarified:
e.g. 13 July — dictate *'13 July — Typist, that is
one three'*.

SPECIAL INSTRUCTIONS TO SECRETARY/TYPIST

In order that the secretary/typist can sort out what he
or she actually has to type as text, and what are your
instructions, you will need to agree a procedure between
you.

This is called an 'arresting instruction', i.e. use
secretary's name or say *'Typist'* or *'Typist, please'*. He or
she will then stop and listen for your *special instructions*:

'Jill I would like the next three paragraphs inset and numbered'
'. . . the "excessive" demands made on . . .'
dictate — *'the, Typist, open quotes — excessive — close quotes
demands made on . . .'*
not — *'the excessive, that's in quotes please'*
'. . . the attached example (Appendix 1) shows . . .'

dictate — '*the attached example, Typist — open brackets — Appendix 1 — close brackets, shows . . .*'

UNDERLINING

Instructions for underlining words will depend on whether the secretary/typist is using a typewriter or a word processor.

Word processor — give instruction before dictating the word:

> e.g. excessive demands
> dictate — '*Jill, underline the next two words please — excessive demands*'

Typewriter — give the instruction after dictating the words:

> e.g. dictate '*excessive demands, Typist, underline last two words please*'

Please establish with your secretary/typist what special instructions he or she requires and in which order he or she needs them, i.e. headings, bold type.

USE OF CAPITAL LETTERS

There will be occasions when the secretary/typist will need help in the use of capital letters — remember he or she is not a mind reader:

> e.g. We are looking at the Capital Loan Fund to see if there are . . .
> dictate — '*we are looking at the — Typist, initial capitals please — Capital Loan Fund (then pause) to see if there are . . .*'

An experienced audio typist will understand that all the words between your instruction and the pause are to have initial capital letters:

> *Not* — 'we are looking at the capital loan fund — that's capital C capital L and capital F — to see if there are . . .'
> *Nor* — 'we are looking at the Capital C Capital, Capital L Loan and Capital F Fund to see if there are . . .'

Both are very confusing and extremely time consuming.

You may have required the same words typed as follows — CAPITAL LOAN FUND

> dictate — 'we are looking at the — *Typist, block capitals, please* — CAPITAL LOAN FUND (then pause) *to see if there are* . . .'

Note: instructions for the use of initial capital letters will not be required before dictating names, towns, countries, etc., nor at the beginning of sentences or paragraphs.

Golden rule — when you want to dictate a special instruction always use an 'arresting instruction' so that the secretary/typist will stop typing text.

It is very important that the secretary/typist understands 'arresting instructions' so you will need to agree them between you.

INSTRUCTIONS AT THE END OF EACH PIECE OF DICTATION

Tell the secretary/typist — End of letter, of memo, etc . . .'

> — 'Next item is . . .'

Depending on the type of index slip or typing requisition form you use you may need to add verbal instructions after each piece of dictation:

> e.g. *'Jill, could you type a label, not an envelope, as there are a number of enclosures*
> *'Typist, as this is a confidential memo, please return it to me in a sealed A4 envelope — thank you.'*

INSTRUCTIONS AT THE END OF TAPE

Tell the secretary/typist — *'End of dictation on this tape'*

DON'T FORGET to say *'thank you'* — (remember he or she is human.)

Check with your own secretary/typist if he or she requires you to run the tape back to the beginning. This will vary — some like to see how much work there is on the tape; also, if you are using a pocket machine this operation will run the battery down.

ERRORS

When we write out text for typing we cross out our mistakes with pen or pencil and insert the new word. A shorthand typist is also able to change your words in the shorthand book when you change your mind. The same principle applies to mistakes we make on tapes. All audio machines are designed to enable us to correct errors.

Remember — good audio dictation means never having to say sorry on tape.

CORRECTING MISTAKES

How to correct the mistake you realise you have just made as you are dictating:

> e.g.'. . . the meeting on Thursday, 24 May sorry that should be Wednesday'

When you realise you have made a mistake — STOP. Run the tape back — listen to what you have said — stop at the last natural pause before your error — continue in record mode — repeat the phrase including the correct word. (Listening to the tape no-one would ever know you made the mistake in the first place.)

When you realise you have made a mistake at the end of a piece of dictation:

> e.g. you have finished the letter and the mistake about Thursday 24 May was in the first paragraph. You would be extremely lucky if you ran the tape back to the error and managed to dictate the new word without erasing others. It is also very time consuming and there are easier ways.

Do not use the tape to inform the secretary/typist of the error:

> e.g. *'Jill, that's the end of the letter — sorry — could you change Thursday to Wednesday in first paragraph.'*

Do put an indication in red on the index slip accompanying the tape so that the secretary/typist is aware of the change before typing.

Check your own audio system — some systems enable users to indicate mechanically any instructions. The secretary/typist is then able to insert the tape into the transcribe machine and fast forward the tape to hear any instructions before typing.

With so many secretaries/typists now using WPs you might be asking why we need to go to all this bother. With the aid of this book we are aiming to become good dictators on tape. Whilst acknowledging it is easy to correct mistakes on WPs I would encourage tape users to aim for perfection as much as possible.

Once you have acquired bad habits it is harder to break them. You might not always work in a company where your tapes are transcribed on WPs.

Remember — the other half of the team — the secretary/typist, who is also proud of the work he or she produces — constantly making corrections which are not his or her fault is frustrating and breaks the typing rhythm. Again, it is time consuming.

Finally, during the dictation of a tape you should playback to yourself and check for:

- clarity

- volume

- pace

- background noise.

USING BOTH SIDES OF THE TAPE

If you have to use both sides of the tape there are certain things to remember that towards the end of side one you will hear a signal warning you that the end of the tape is approaching. Do not dictate through this signal. Stop at a convenient point and tell the secretary/typist:

'End of dictation on this side — I will continue on the other side of the tape.'

On the other side, you will now need to re-introduce yourself and remind the secretary/typist:

'This is the continuation from first side.'

This is a safety measure in case he or she puts the wrong side of the tape into the machine and starts on the second side.

CHECKLIST 1

WHAT DO WE SEND TO THE SECRETARY/TYPIST WITH THE TAPE?

INDEX SLIPS

- to show name of dictator, date, how many items and what they are

- to include any corrections, special instructions.

Priority tapes suitably marked for speed of identification.

Any previous correspondence (in a folder in correct order for typing) will save you spelling addresses, names, etc.

Any tabulations or work to be included from copy (if in files flag up the appropriate pages).

Any precedents to indicate particular layouts, i.e. reports, minutes.

Any enclosures.

Put the tape into an envelope inside a folder or attach to the slip or typing requisition form.

Tapes are small and can easily get lost; there is no way of telling by looking at the tape if there is work on it that needs to be transcribed or if it is dead.

Always establish with your secretary/typist the procedure for cleaning tapes after they have been transcribed. All transcribe machines have the facility to wipe tapes clean.

CHECKLIST 2

RULES TO REMEMBER

1 Understand the machine and the controls.
2 Establish with secretary/typist what information he or she needs.
3 Choose a quiet place to dictate and be aware of background noises.
4 Sort out work into routine and priority dictation.
5 Use specially marked tapes for PRIORITY work.
6 Obtain all necessary files and information and keep them handy.
7 Plan what you are going to say — make notes.
8 Complete index slip as you go through tape.
9 Dictate clearly in a natural voice.
10 Never allow the tape to run on when not dictating.
11 Get the dictation to flow — stopping and starting makes the tape sound disjointed.
12 When stopping tape, do not clip off last word.
13 Always start at the beginning of the tape.
14 If using both sides of tape, re-introduce yourself.
15 Treat secretary/typist like a human being — use his or her name if possible.
16 Remember all instructions you are required to give.
17 Always correct mistakes.
18 Notify the end of each item of dictation and end of dictation on tape.
19 Send tape in envelope or attached to index slip.
20 Regularly check your own dictation — play back tapes.
21 Check tapes and batteries regularly.
22 Listen to the feedback from secretary/typist.

Remember practice makes perfect.

CHECKLIST 3

PRONUNCIATION

Take care when dictating the following:

All words ending in -ents or -ence
All word participles ending in -ed

accede/exceed	forth/fourth
access/excess	forward/foreword
addition/edition	incite/insight
advise/advice	it's/its
affect/effect	legislator/legislature
allusion/illusion	licence/license
Arran/Arun	lightening/lightning
assistance/assistants	lose/loose
bite/byte	mendacity/mendicity
canvas/canvass	minor/miner
cease/seize	ordnance/ordinance
check/cheque	overseas/oversees
cite/sight/site	palette/palate
coarse/course	passed/past
compliment/complement	personal/personnel
council/counsel	petition/partition
deceased/diseased	practice/practise
decent/descent	practical/practicable
defer/differ	precedence/precedents
dependent/(upon)	principle/principal
/dependant(retainer)	proceed/precede
disapprove/disprove	programme/program
discreet/discrete	prophesy/prophecy
elicit/illicit	respectfully/respectively
eligible/illegible	rite/right/write
emigrate/immigrate	stationery/stationary
eminent/imminent	straight/strait
era/error	their/there/they're
finely/finally	Ulster/Alcester
fiscal/physical	we are tempted/we
formally/formerly	attempted

WRITING SKILLS

Good writing is writing that works. It is clear at first reading: it demands no further explanation.

For most of us, writing is not something that comes easily. In the age of video and the telephone, it can seem an old–fashioned, unnatural way to communicate. Yet the demand for words on paper grows: letters, memos, faxes, reports, minutes of meetings, marketing copy, procedures, manuals . . .

The good news is that effective writing is a skill which can be learnt. The written word, though, can be intimidating, and it's worth considering briefly some of the problems that people bring to the task.

"I LACK CONFIDENCE"

Some people seem to be gifted with the ability to write well. The impression can be deceptive. The French philosopher Pascal once wrote a letter to a friend apologising for its length: "*I lack the time,*" he wrote, "*to make it shorter.*"

Good writing is always the result of hard work. The reason is simple: we are not there to help with gesture or tone of voice — with the force of our personality. Anything we write must act on our behalf.

What's more, words on paper can seem fixed and unchangeable: the written word has an objectivity and a sense of authority which can be threatening.

We have to do everything we can to take command: to stop written English frightening us.

"THE MATERIAL'S TOO COMPLICATED"

— or: *"I don't know what to include and what to leave out."*
    This problem usually arises because:

- we have not thought clearly about the message we want to send;

- we are not thinking about the reader, only the information we have to put down;

- we may be more concerned about what will look impressive;

- we may not be able to concentrate on the job in hand.

The result of all this is:

- muddled thinking:

- a muddled structure (because our thinking is muddled):

- language that goes out of control.

So there are two golden rules that every writer must bear in mind:

Think of the reader.

All writing should focus on the reader **before** the material to be included.

Separate thinking from writing

Writing's hard enough as it is, without trying to think at the same time! We must put our thoughts in order before we begin, and take time afterwards to think about what we have written.

"I KNOW WHAT I WANT TO SAY, BUT I CAN'T PUT IT DOWN . . ."

If we were speaking, we would know exactly how to put it; but, when it comes to putting it on paper, it just won't travel from head to hand.

This is probably because we think that written English should be somehow different: more 'formal', more 'proper'. The answer is: write as you speak. Your text can be improved later.

"I WAFFLE"

So waffle! At least your writing will have some sort of flow, and not be stilted or impersonal. Good writing comes from **rewriting,** when waffle can be extracted; but if you are so unconfident that you write nothing, what will there be to rewrite?

"I DON'T HAVE TIME TO IMPROVE"

— or: "*There's always too much to do,*" or "*It's got to be right first time.*"

Nonsense. No piece of writing **ever** comes out right at the first attempt. Of course time is short: our task as writers is to manage it better.

We must allow time to prepare, and time to check. That way our text **will** be right first time — the first time the reader sees it.

"THERE'S NO POINT IN ANY OF THIS: MY BOSS CORRECTS EVERYTHING ANYWAY"

This is a very difficult problem to solve. Nobody can write in somebody else's style (unless they are a satirist). Briefly, if a person is given the authority to write a document, he or she should be allowed to write it his or her way.

Everybody can improve the way they write, and help from a trusted colleague can be invaluable. Nothing is more dispiriting, however, than a red pen wielded insensitively.

In the age of the 'flatter' organisation, language used to assert position within a hierarchy is becoming increasingly out of date. Departments and teams need to speak — and write — clearly to one another; organisations must demonstrate their sense of accountability to the public by using language that **everybody** understands.

A SYSTEMATIC APPROACH

Any piece of writing should be tackled systematically, in three stages:

- **PREPARATION AND PLANNING**

- **WRITING**

- **CHECKING**

PREPARATION

The best way to prepare writing is to ask a series of basic questions:

- Why?

- Who?

- When?

- Where?

- What?

- How?

Certain fundamental issues must be clarified before we proceed.

WHY?

What is the purpose of the document we are writing?

Try to write that purpose down, as a simple verbal phrase: *"To. . ."*

A letter may be written to give information, to answer a complaint, or to demand action. A report's purpose may be to persuade, to justify expenditure, or to recommend a series of actions. A manual's purpose will be to instruct the user; a marketing brochure's to sell a product or service.

If your document seems to have more than one purpose, pick one and stick to it. A piece of writing which tries to do too much at once will fail to do anything.

Remember that all documents carrying your organisation's name are free advertisements. Every document should act to promote both its writer and the organisation from which it comes.

WHO?

We would not speak to an invisible audience; we should never write without having a reader in mind.

What do we know about our reader? What do they want? What do they need? What do **they** know? What are their attitudes, skills, even prejudices?

WHO? ME?

You must take responsibility for your writing. Your name will probably go on it. Are you the right person for the job? Do you have access to the right information? Above all, do you have the authority to write what you want to write?

WHERE?

What is the document's destination? Within the department? To another organisation?

Where, too, will you write? Is it quiet and free from interruption? If not: can you manage anywhere better?

WHEN?

Establish clear deadlines: at both ends, for you and the reader. Establish a working schedule and stick to it. Try to write when your mind is clearest. The best work of the day can sometimes be done before breakfast.

WHAT?

What material do I put in? What is relevant to my purpose — and to my reader? What have I got? What else do I need? Where will I go to find it? How do I collect it?

The answers to these questions may be very simple; or they may take months to find. Either way, there will come a point when you will want to gather your material together and organise it into a sequence that is logical and persuasive.

Perhaps you will make a list. You may extract what you think are the 'keypoints' and try to put them in order with material listed under each.

The problem is that lists rarely come out right first time, and must be redrafted — sometimes over and over again. Even when they finally seem correct, we are left with the lingering doubt that something has been left out.

The reason is that lists give our material a predetermined order, automatically giving the items at the top an importance they may not deserve. By writing a list we commit ourselves to a single train of thought. Lists are like tramlines, limiting our thinking.

PATTERN PLANS: AN EXAMPLE

Pattern plans are an increasingly popular method of organising information. They allow us to access information by making associative as well as logical connections.

To construct a pattern plan:

- Take a **plain** sheet of paper and draw a circle in the middle.

- Write down the subject to be considered in the circle — or draw a picture which suggests the subject to you.

229

- Write down any ideas connected with the subject — in any order. Omit nothing!

- Highlight the 'key' ideas, using different colours.

- Group information around these key ideas using 'branches' and 'twigs'. Add and edit items; probably only a few will have to be moved.

- Continue until the pattern plan is complete.

- List the key ideas as headings, with information under each, in a logical sequence.

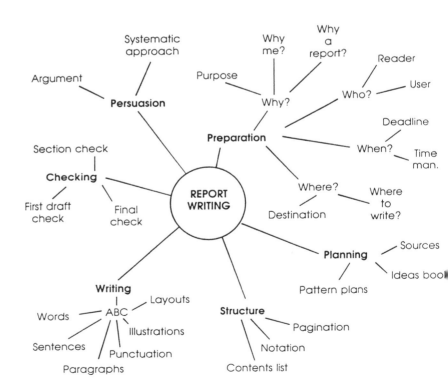

This may seem like aimless daydreaming. In fact, daydreaming is one of the most creative forms of thinking. Pattern plans harness our creativity and link it to our powers of logic. They have a number of advantages as thinking tools:

- *rapidity:* more ideas in a shorter time;
- *completeness:* we can see the whole on one sheet of paper and omissions will be easier to spot;
- *efficiency:* a pattern plan gathers and structures material **simultaneously;**
- *individuality:* this is **our** record thinking. If it makes sense to us, it is much more likely to make sense to the reader.

Each group on the plan will form the basis of a section or paragraph of the finished document.

We are now throughly prepared: we know why we are writing, and we have a clear structure to follow. Now we can begin to write!

WRITING

Remember: this is the easy part. The task is to produce a first draft. This is not the time for thinking hard: it is the time to try to let the words flow onto the page.

- Write fast. Try at all costs to avoid being interrupted. Stick to your plan: don't be tempted to fiddle with it.
- Write as you speak. Listen to the words in your head: put them down as you hear them.

CHECKING

Checking the first draft is a vital stage in the writing process. Good writing comes from rewriting: it is now that we analyse thoroughly what we have written and create a text that is correct, clear and appropriate — to our purpose, and to our reader.

Analysing our own writing can be difficult: it is much easier to rewrite somebody else's text. Somehow we have to develop the skill of reading our writing critically, as if somebody else had written it.

Try to allow some time between finishing the draft and beginning to check it. The longer the better; but even an hour spent on something else will give us a certain level of objectivity.

Remember: there is no such thing as a final version. Rewriting is an endless process, limited only by time. As usual, a systematic approach will work best.

CHECKING: A 10-POINT PLAN

Follow this procedure in order. It checks the major factors first and proceeds to smaller details. Rewriting is often a matter of changing lots of little things rather than a few big ones.

1. PARAGRAPHS

Paragraphs present one aspect of a subject. They may have more than one sentence; they will only ever have one theme.

- Check each page of the document. If a page has fewer than two paragraph breaks, try to put in more.

- Use short paragraphs to summarise at the beginning and end of each section or document.

- Isolate action points in their own paragraphs.

- Break long paragraphs into shorter sections, using sub-headings, numbers or lists. Be consistent in your layout.

- Open each paragraph with a short, summarising **topic sentence.** It should be possible to speed-read these topic sentences and pick up the gist of the whole text.

- Use link words and phrases to guide the reader from one paragraph to the next:

  However . . .
  Moreover . . .
  As a result . . .
  In addition . . .
  In contrast . . .
  — and so on.

2. LONG SENTENCES

A sentence can be described as a group of words which makes sense by itself. It begins with a CAPITAL LETTER and ends with a STOP (full stop; exclamation mark; question mark).

Short sentences are easier to read than long ones. This does not mean, however, that every sentence we write should be four words long! The average sentence length in modern English is about 17 words. A sentence of 25 words or over will probably not be understood at first reading.

Sentences tend to grow out of control because we try to cram too many ideas into them. The only answer is to separate thought from writing.

● Use your shortest sentences in the most prominent positions. The bigger the idea, the shorter the sentence to express it.

● Search out your long sentences (25 words or more). Rewrite them in the following way:

1. List the ideas in the sentence, reordering if necessary to make logical sense.
2. Rewrite each idea as a separate sentence.
3. Connect into prose, using link words or phrases.
4. Check the language of the rewritten text and cut it down if necessary.

3. SUBJECT AND VERB

Every sentence must have a SUBJECT. Grammatically, the subject will always be a NOUN (the table; the company; satisfaction; John; September; Essex).

It must also have a MAIN VERB, which describes what the subject is or does. The verb must agree with the subject (singular or plural), and it must be FINITE, having TENSE (past, present, future, etc.).

● If in doubt, ask:

– What do you want the sentence to be **about?**
– Put this at the very beginning as the subject.
– What is the subject doing? Put that second. Put nothing between subject and verb. Now rewrite the sentence from there.

4. SENTENCE LANDSCAPE

Normally we don't read one word at a time. The eye scans in groups of about five words, searching through the sentence for the full stop which tells it to pause.

- Put the most important ideas at the beginning or end of each sentence, where attention is greatest. Ideas buried in the middle will risk being lost.

- Try to break long sentences into manageable 'chunks' of between five and ten words.

5. PASSIVE AND ACTIVE VERBS

Beware of writing *impersonally:*

> *Arrangements have been made . . .*
> *Measurements were taken . . .*
> *All letters should be addressed . . .*

This use of the **passive voice** lacks the personal tone that is the mark of good business relations. It complicates the document's language and, most importantly, can fail to allocate responsibility for actions taken.

- Turn passive verbs into **active verbs,** which tell the reader who is doing what:

> *I have made arrangements . . .*
> *The field team took measurements . . .*
> *Please address all letters to . . .*

6. ADJECTIVES AND ADVERBS

Adjectives describe nouns (quick; yellow; round; cold; happy); **adverbs** describe verbs (quickly; brightly; separately; early). Adverbs sometimes also describe adjectives (*quite* fast; *rather* hot).

- Go through your text, identifying the adjectives and adverbs. Take them all out and see which are absolutely necessary.

7. ACCURACY

Accuracy means using the right word for the right job. Remember that words can change their meanings over time, or according to their context. Words disappear from use: terms appropriate thirty years ago may now seem old-fashioned. New words can appear almost overnight.

- Use *jargon* in its rightful place — between experts. If writing for non-specialists, avoid it or take care to give an explanation.

8. BREVITY

- Use short words rather than long ones wherever possible.

- Eliminate meaningless cliches:

  As a matter of fact
  As such
  By and large
  For your information
  Needless to say

- Watch out for *tautology.* Why say the same thing twice?

  He declined to accept our offer.
  Enclosed herewith . . .
  The true facts are . . .

9. CLARITY

Clarity is the hallmark of plain English. Remember that we are not there to explain what we have written: the text must leave no room for ambiguity.

- **Vague phrases** can arouse suspicion:

  in the region of
  in the area of
  around about
  Are we covering up something unpleasant, or
  hiding our ignorance?

- **Loaded words** convey value judgements we may
  not have intended. During a survey, members of
  the public may have been **approached, asked a
  question, questioned, interviewed,** or even
  interrogated. What idea do we want to convey —
  precisely?

- The greatest threat to clarity comes from **abstract
  nouns.**

  **There are regulations for the avoidance of
  accidents.**
  Satisfaction is guaranteed.
  Your entitlement to a refund is unaffected.

  Abstract nouns can very often be replaced by the
  verbs from which they derive:

  The rules help us to avoid accidents.
  We know you will be satisfied.
  You are still entitled to a refund.

  Abstract nouns can mean different things to
  different people. Concrete words simplify the
  language and probably mean much the same to the
  reader as they do to you.

Ipso facto, we have not found your umbrella per se, but we will search ad infinitum.

10. SPELLING AND PUNCTUATION

Spelling matters. Like it or not, it contributes to our public and professional image.

Take heart! English is notoriously inconsistent, and everybody has some difficulties with spelling. There are ways of improving — if you are determined.

- Think before you write. Clear thoughts make for clear writing.

- Use the simpler, shorter word rather than the longer, complicated one. ***Always.***

- Don't use any word unfamiliar to you. You are more likely to spell correctly words you know.

- Make a point of looking up new words in a dictionary and becoming acquainted with them.

- If in doubt: write it down quickly. First guesses are often correct. However:

- *Never* rely on guesses. Check with the dictionary.

- Use a *good* dictionary: one that is difficult to lift!

- Never rely on the dictionary on your WP. It will not be comprehensive, and may include American spellings.

- Beware too the spellchecker: it will not recognise the difference between **there** and **their,** or between **modern** and **modem.**

- Keep a notebook for words that refuse to stick in the mind. Note down misspellings and new words, and take a few minutes every day to check yourself against the list.

- Use a thesaurus to expand your vocabulary.

Punctuation does for the written word what gesture, pausing and tone of voice do for speech. It signals to the reader how to read the passage.

- Keep it simple! The less punctuation, the better.

- Read your text aloud, checking that the punctuation does what it should. Remove any unnecessary punctuation; add only when you are convinced you should.

- Never use any punctuation without being sure of its use.

- Check the finer points of punctuation in a guide to usage.

The following sections detail the procedures for specific kinds of documents:

- **Letters**

- **Reports**

•Agendas and Minutes

The rules of plain English apply to all of them. We are not writing to impress — or to win the Nobel Prize! The documents we produce have a job to do: they will do it better if the language we use is clear, concise and correct.

1. LETTER WRITING

A letter is a piece of conversation by post. It expresses a relationship: between friends, colleagues, or total strangers. The nature of the relationship dictates the nature of the letter.

Letters have come to be seen as a rather formal way to communicate. 'Formal', though, does not mean 'impersonal'. We are responsible for every letter we sign: legally, and professionally; and in business letter-writing the personal element is increasingly regarded as of crucial importance.

An effective business letter is precise, straightforward, relevant to the reader's needs, and — above all — action-centred. It shows respect for the reader and points the way ahead, saying clearly what happens next.

Writing letters is a time-consuming business — and time is money. A business letter can cost upwards of £20 to produce. By adopting a systematic approach, we can use the limited time at our disposal more efficiently, and produce letters that are personal, professional and effective.

PREPARATION

THE BASIC QUESTIONS

Even a short letter requires preparation. Time spent now, before putting pen to paper, is time saved later — both for you, and for your reader.

WHY? THE LETTER'S PURPOSE

Every letter, even the most routine, has a purpose.

Try to establish the reason for writing your letter. Write it down as a simple verbal phrase. For example:

- **To sell or persuade**

- **To make an enquiry**

- **To answer a question**

- **To complain**

- **To answer a complaint**

- **To get something done**

- **To create a good impression of ourselves and our organisation**

All these **statements of purpose** are action-centred.

If a letter seems to have more than one purpose, pick the most important one and stick to it. A letter which tries to do too much will fail to do anything.

Remember that all letters should strive to give a good impression. Every letter we send is a free advertisement.

It is also worth asking, at this stage: "Why am I writing a letter?" A telephone call might clarify matters more quickly — and more cheaply. A letter, on the other hand, can provide a structured explanation of complicated information, and can be kept as a permanent record.

Urgency may dictate the use of a fax. Remember, though, that the time saved in sending the document is extra time for thinking and writing. A fax needs as much attention as any other document. Similarly with electronic mail: don't be seduced by the technology into sloppiness which could cause problems and delays later.

WHO IS THE READER?

What we put in our letter — and what we leave out — will depend on our relationship with the reader.

- Do we know his or her name — exactly? This may be difficult to find out, but it is worth the effort.

- Is he or she the right person? Is he or she in a position to take the action we require? All our work may be wasted if our letter is opened by the wrong person, particularly in a large organisation.

- What are his or her needs? What does he or she want? Is there a conflict between the two?

- What does he or she know about us and our organisation? Does the situation have a 'history'? Does our organisation have a particular public image or reputation? How can we turn our reader's probable attitudes to our advantage?

- What does the reader know about the subject of the letter? We may be writing to a well-known colleague, or to a member of the public; to an expert, or a child. The words we use will vary accordingly.

- Will our letter have more than one reader? Mailshots and standard letters must be drafted carefully. We may need to break our readership into groups, with different letters for each.

WHO? ME?

Am I the right person to write this letter? Perhaps liaising with other organisations, or with the public, is part of my job; perhaps I regard letters as an occasional and annoying interruption of my 'real' work.

Remember that the person signing the letter is legally responsible for it, even when signing 'pp' or on behalf of another — unless the signature is accompanied by the disclaimer: "Dictated by . . . and signed in their absence."

Letters are all too often delegated to writers whose work is then mercilessly 'corrected' by the person whose signature appears at the bottom. Nothing destroys a writer's confidence more surely than a manager's red pen wielded without explanation. In general, the writer of the letter should have the authority to sign it; and the person who signs should take on the responsibility of writing. If neither of these is possible, close collaboration and mutual respect of each other's style is essential.

WHEN?

Letters take time to arrive. Be realistic when allowing time for delivery and reply. Take into account also the reader's schedule or deadlines.

Be aware of the methods of despatch available to you. Important letters are worth signalling by phone; faxes should certainly be accompanied by a call to the recipient.

WHERE?

All your hard work will be wasted if the letter gets lost! Make sure the address is accurate, complete and up-to-date.

Give thought, too, to where you will be writing. It really should be somewhere quiet, convenient, and conducive to concentration. Don't feel bound to your desk; ten minutes' quiet thought elsewhere can be ten minutes well spent — especially if you are stuck for words.

PLANNING

What will happen as a result of your letter?

Your statement of purpose centres on a future action, either by you, or by the reader. The **action point** of the letter is whatever needs to be done to fulfil the letter's purpose.

- What action is required? By whom? When?
- What information is relevant to the action point?
- What does the reader already know?
- What do I know?
- What else do I need to know?

Use a pattern plan to gather this information together and plan the letter. Each group of items will form the basis for a paragraph. The items for each paragraph are logically ordered and omissions are obvious — before you've even begun to write!

STRUCTURE

Every letter needs a structure: it saves time and confusion.

The material in almost all business letters follows this basic format:

- **Salutation**

- **Heading**

- **Introduction**

- **Body**

- **Action point**

- **Concluding remarks**

- **The complimentary close and signature**

SALUTATION

The etiquette of letter-writing has relaxed in recent years, and a few basic rules will suffice.

- Use the reader's name if you know it. The form of the name will depend on how they have addressed you or signed themselves, or on how well you know them. Business contacts, even if they have never previously communicated, now increasingly use first names:

Dear Gillian . . .
Dear Freddie . . .

The more formal style of salutation is normally reserved for customers or members of the public:

Dear Mr Magee . . .
Dear Mrs Ikoli . . .

- If the marital status of a female reader is unclear, and you feel you cannot use her first name, we recommend the use of **Ms.**

- If you cannot find out your reader's name, you might use a job title:

  Dear Production Manager . . .
  Dear Headteacher . . .

- As a last resort, you may have to use:

  Dear Sir . . .
  Dear Madam . . .
  Dear Sir or Madam . . .

  But avoid these if at all possible. These, and any other form of salutation, are impersonal and unfriendly. They no longer denote a 'business style'; they merely show lack of personal attention to the reader.

HEADING

All business letters benefit from a heading. Go back to your statement of purpose for ideas.

Make sure your heading is short but meaningful. **Invoice No 876230** may mean nothing: **Installation of new kitchen units** is more helpful.

Place the heading between the salutation and the introduction. A heading makes it much easier to start the letter with a short first sentence:

DELIVERIES OF SMOKELESS FUEL
Thank you for your enquiry.

RE: SITING OF STREET LAMPS IN TURL STREET
Many thanks for your helpful remarks.

INTRODUCTION

The first paragraph of your letter should identify:

- an acknowledgement of any previous communication (with date);

- who the writer is (job title);

- why you are writing.

Take care to avoid opening letters in ways that are verbose, old-fashioned or grammatically incorrect:

In reply to your letter of . . .
With reference to your telephone conversation of . . .
Further to your complaint registered on . . .
Your letter has been passed to me as Quality Controller . . .

Begin simply and politely:

Thank you for your letter of 4 April.
I was interested to read your comments on . . .

Beware of stating the obvious:

I am writing to inform you . . .

A reference to what you want, or are about to do, creates a much more interesting and individual opening:

I am concerned . . .
I am interested in . . .
We met recently at the conference on . . .
I would like to introduce myself in my new post as . . .

BODY

This is the meat of the letter.

- Ensure that all the material is relevant to the action point and logically ordered.

- Give paragraphs sub–headings or numbers if necessary.

- Summarise each paragraph with a short, **topic sentence.**

- Use bullet points for information which can be listed.

ACTION POINT

This is the most important part! If the reader misses this, your letter will have failed.

Isolate the action point by placing it in its own paragraph. If appropriate, use bold type or italics.

Any action point should indicate:

- what action is to be taken (at your end or the reader's);

- when it is to be taken;

- who is responsible for taking it.

Be careful not to be too abrupt in your demands, or too effusive in your promises. Actions should be specific and realistic.

CONCLUDING REMARKS

The last sentence of the letter is as important as the first. You are setting the seal on the relationship, and pointing the way forward.

Avoid the stale and standard conclusion:

Assuring you of our best attention . . .
In the meantime, if you have any queries, please do not hesitate to contact me . . .

These remarks, and others like them, have become such clichés that the reader will not know whether they are genuine or not. You can be polite *and* genuine:

I am this address if you have any questions.
I look forward to meeting you.
Please call me on . . . if you need help.

Think about what you would say face to face and write it down. It may need very little adjustment to be acceptable at the end of a letter.

THE COMPLIMENTARY CLOSE AND SIGNATURE

The rule is simple.

Use **Yours sincerely** when you salute the reader by name. Otherwise use **Yours faithfully.** Other complimentary closes will suggest other types of relationships than the strictly professional. Use them at your own risk!

Note the use of capital letters: for **Yours** only.

Sign with your first name if you have saluted the reader by first name; otherwise with your first and last names (NOT an initial and last name).

Print or type your full name below the signature, including a personal title if you wish (**Mr, Mrs, Miss, Ms**). The job title is printed or typed below the printed name. Name or job title — but not both — can be printed in upper case.

Yours sincerely

Michelle Sussams
PERSONNEL DIRECTOR

LAYOUT

However well-written, a letter which is poorly laid out will fail at the first hurdle.

Most business letters come in one of two layouts:

INDENTED

- addresses and close/signature progressively indented;

- heading, writer's name and job title centred;

- closed punctuation (commas and stops in names and addresses, dates, complimentary close).

Now regarded as old-fashioned, mostly because of the complexity of typing. Not recommended.

BLOCKED

- everything starting at the left margin;

- open punctuation (all punctuation omitted outside the main body of the letter).

This is far easier to produce, and is now increasingly accepted as the norm.

WRITING

Once the purpose and structure of your letter is clear, the writing itself becomes much easier.

Beware of writing in a certain way because it seems

more 'proper'. There is no such thing as 'business English': there is only good English. The formality of a letter lies in its structure and a few basic conventions. In every other respect, the language we use should be as close to the spoken word as possible.

CHECKING

Use the 10-point plan to review your first draft. Remember: your letter, if read aloud, should have the sound of your own voice.

TONE

Tone is difficult to define. We all know the wrong tone when we read it: but creating the right tone can be tricky. Remember the three elements of good tone:

BE POSITIVE: BE DEFINITE: BE SINCERE

•Be positive

Always say what you *will* do; not what you can't:

We cannot supply the goods before October.
We will send the goods on 1 October.

•Be definite

Don't promise what you can't deliver:

I will try to hold the tickets for you.
I will hold these tickets for three days.

•Be sincere

Generate the feeling appropriate to your purpose. Don't cloud the message with emotional language which could be interpreted as a personal attack:

Your failure to reply . . .
Your refusal to cooperate . . .
Your repeated and unnecessary correspondence . . .

All these examples should be replaced with language that is sincere but also polite — in a word, professional:

Please reply by the end of the week.
As you feel that you would rather not work on this project . . .
Thank you for your letters about . . .

Before your letter slips into its envelope, take a long hard look at it:

- Does it look good? Is it interesting and easy to read? If it landed on your desk, would you want to read it?

- Does it give a good impression of you, and of your organisation?

- Does it achieve its objective?

- Is the action point clear?

- Is the information accurate, relevant, logically ordered and complete?

- Is the layout correct?

- Is the heading brief but specific?

- Are the paragraphs of manageable length?

- Are there any sentences of 25 words or more? Are the shortest sentences in the most prominent positions?

- Is the language accurate, brief and clear?

- Are the salutation and complimentary close correct?

- Are all relevant enclosures included?

- Have you got copies for everyone who needs them?

- What about grammar, spelling and punctuation?

A good letter is one that does its job well. Once you have adopted a systematic approach you will enjoy the real pleasure of seeing your letters improve. They will become excellent ambassadors for you — and for your organisation.

2. REPORT WRITING

A report is an exercise in persuasion.

The process of making decisions is becoming ever more complex as managerial responsibilities are distributed more and more widely. Reports are part of that process. They are the means by which detailed knowledge is transmitted to those who need it.

A report defines a subject or problem; gathers facts in order to present them as completely as possible; and analyses the facts in order to come to conclusions on which the writer bases certain recommendations.

The task of a report is to present a case. In order to do its job well it must be:

- persuasive
- decisive
- action-centred.

As ever, a systematic approach will ensure that report-writing is a challenge and not a chore.

PREPARATION

WHY?

What is the purpose of the report?

You may have been asked for facts; but probably for a reason. Write that reason down, as a *statement of objective:*

The purpose of this report is to . . .

Until you have determined the purpose of the report, you should not proceed any further. Remember that the report's purpose is not the same as its subject.

The subject of an accident report will be the facts: what happened, and why. The report's purpose may be to instigate safety procedures, to assess legal liability, or to arrange compensation. It may address some or all of these at once.

If necessary, ask the person commissioning the report exactly what is required. Discuss too how it will be used: as a consultation document, a briefing document, a client report, a manual . . .

- Agree the purpose of the report

- Define its terms of reference: what will be covered; what is not within the brief

- Write these down and give a copy to commissioner and writer.

Ask, too: **Why a report?** Might there be a better way of doing the job?

WHO?

Reports have **readers** and **users.**

Readers will read the report from cover to cover. They may not be experts in the field, but they could be senior management with control over budgets.

Report users may be colleagues or specialists with particular needs. They have no time to read the whole thing: they will glance at the summary, conclusions and recommendations, then turn to the contents page and pick out what they want.

Both reader and user must be accommodated. Remember that technical or specialised language will confuse a lay reader; and over-explanation will insult an expert.

PLANNING

Writing reports involves gathering facts. For some, it seems to involve nothing else: their reports are admirably complete, but utterly indigestible.

Facts are sacred; but comment is free. Of course the information in any report must be scrupulously accurate; but you have been *asked* to give your opinions, conclusions and recommendations. This, the subjective element, is as important as the objective one.

You may already have recommendations that your report will attempt to justify: funding for a research project, a plan to reorganise a department. Or perhaps you are setting out into the unknown and your recommendations will only become clear as you compile the report.

TERMS OF REFERENCE

These — sometimes called the parameters or scope of the report — are the factors influencing the method of research and the nature of the report. They will include:

- What aspects of the subject are you covering?
  - particular geographical area
  - limited period of time
  - part of an organisation
  - requirements of a specific client
  - contribution to a discussion or meeting

- Deadline for the report

- Available budget

- Distribution list

- Confidentiality

- Internal politics

- Possible methods of research

Information can be gathered from numerous sources:

- organised surveys, questionnaires and interviews;

- in-house documents, minutes of meetings, technical data, and past reports;

- company literature, publicity material and computerised information;

- newspapers, journals, books, theses and articles.

Even the simplest report will include a certain amount of information, gathered over a period of time. It is best to sort the material as you go.

An *ideas book* keeps a record of the material in one place. It also saves time by encouraging preliminary sorting.

It should be hard-backed, A4 size, opened to give an A3 spread.

Rule each page as follows:

Category 1 material is mainstream information, and will become part of the main text.

Category 2 is not essential to your argument, but may be useful as back-up, or for particular report users. It will include statistics, analysis or detailed explanation. It will go into an appendix.

Category 3 is interesting but of doubtful usefulness. You cannot see any place for it at the moment, but are loath to let it go. It goes to one side and may eventually be discarded.

As research progresses, material may move between categories. Details in Category 1 will go into Category 2 for inclusion in an appendix; your hunch that something in Category 3 is actually crucial to your case will result in a move to Category 1.

Use pattern plans at any stage to organise the material in your mind. Be guided by:

- the report's purpose

- the readers and/or users

- any recommendations you are working towards

Put them on the wall to refer to, and add to, over time.

STRUCTURE

Some reports are produced on prepared forms: visit reports and site reports, for example. You may be constrained by a standard format or a client's particular request. Scientific and technical reports follow clear structural conventions. Sometimes organisations have established procedures.

Most formal business reports will follow a similar structure:

- *Title page*
- *Acknowledgements*
- *Summary*
- *Contents page*
- *Introduction*
- *Findings*
- *Conclusions*
- *Recommendations*
- *Appendices*
- *References*
- *Bibliography*
- *Index*

Work on a table of contents before anything else. This will:

- clarify your thinking;
- allow for flexibility;
- give a colleague a chance to check your logic;

- make for quicker writing;

- allow you to write sections in any order;

- give you the satisfaction of seeing the whole report on one page

It is essential to think in terms of **sections:** they are the framework into which the information will be fitted, like rooms in a house that in time will be furnished. Without clearly defined sections, the report will lack cohesion.

The contents list should go on a separate page unless very short. It should include the title of every section and sub-section, including Appendices. A separate list for illustrations is a good idea where a large number are included.

Check your contents list regularly:

- Are headings **accurate?** Do they cover everything within the section?

- Are they **brief** — no more than three or four words?

- Are they **clear?** "Introduction" may not mean much to your reader.

- Do they follow a logical order? "Recommendations", for example, should follow "Conclusions".

- Are the sub-headings clear?

- Is there a gap in the logical progression of ideas? A section missing?

- Too many sub-headings in one section?

- Any section too short? Can it be amalgamated within another?

- Do you have material for every section? More research required?

- Is every section necessary?

NOTATION

Decimal numbering is generally recognised to be the most straightforward method of notation. It shows more clearly than any other the hierarchy of your thoughts:

Section	*1*
Sub-section	*1.1*
Paragraph	*1.1.1*
	1.1.2
Sub-section	*1.2*
Section	*2*

Three sub-divisions should prove quite sufficient: if you run to four or more, you risk confusing the reader. Restructure the section.

Every section of the report should be notated in this way, apart from the contents page itself and the summary, which will not be notated; and any Appendices, which are usually identified by capital letters and numbers (A.1 . . . B.1 . . .).

PAGE NUMBERS

It is common practice to leave the title page unnumbered and to number every page before the Introduction with roman numerals (*i, ii, iii, iv, . . .*)

The best way of paginating thereafter is to number pages within sections. Section 1 will run from page 1/1, Section 2 from 2/1 and so on. This is particularly helpful if you are not writing the report in order; it will also accommodate additions ('3/4a') and deletions ('no page 5/2').

Appendices are paginated similarly but with letters instead of numbers: A/1, A/2 and so on.

INTRODUCTION

This includes:

- Terms of reference
- Background: how the report came into being; who commissioned it
- Objectives: purpose, intended uses
- Methodology
- Arrangement of material in the report

FINDINGS

Or 'body', or 'discussion'. This is your evidence. Opinions, conclusions and recommendations have no place here.

Use language to present the information persuasively. Remember: you are pursuing an argument.

CONCLUSIONS

The order of your conclusions should follow the order of the findings.

Conclusions are your considered opinion based on your analysis of the evidence. Never introduce new evidence at this stage. If the research is sound, you should have no fear of expressing your conclusions unambiguously.

RECOMMENDATIONS

This is the most important part of the report.

Recommendations should be specific, measurable, and achievable. Be sure to allocate responsibility for any actions you recommend. Give names and deadlines.

If there is a range of options: don't hedge. State your preferred course of action. Advise, urge: you must convince your reader that you are right. If you cannot make the decision (because you don't have the authority), make it clear who must decide. Don't be afraid, even then, to state a preference.

APPENDICES

Here is the detailed information required by some users but not all: statistics, diagrams, charts, graphs, computer print-outs, extracts from magazines.

ACKNOWLEDGEMENTS AND GLOSSARY

Acknowledgements acting as PR — thanking a sponsor, for example — are certainly best placed at or near the beginning of a report. A glossary, too, can be welcome before the text proper. Otherwise place them after the Appendices. Include them in the contents list.

REFERENCES AND BIBLIOGRAPHY

By convention, References usually precede Bibliography.

References are to material specifically referred to, or quoted, in the text. At the point of reference in the text, they are marked with a number, perhaps in square brackets; the numbers are then listed in order in this section. Each reference will include author, title, place and date of publication, and page number.

The *Bibliography* lists material not referred to in the report but which may be of interest. Items in the Bibliography are set out exactly similarly to references, but are listed alphabetically by name of author. They are unnumbered.

Begin these lists as soon as it becomes clear you will need them. Nothing is more tedious than assembling them after the report is complete!

WRITING A SUMMARY

Readers will use the summary to give a sense of what the whole report is about, or to remind them of its main points. Users will want to know how 'their' bit fits into the whole.

Summaries are beginning to take on an increasingly independent role. They will be read by people who may never see the report at all but want to know what's going on in the department. Decision-makers may look only at the summary to tell them what to do. Research suggests that the vast majority of managers only ever read report summaries.

For these reasons, writers sometimes produce general or **management summaries,** and **executive summaries** stressing recommendations and actions.

The summary page should always include:

- the report title and author
- date
- reference number
- any indication of confidentiality

The summary is obviously the final part of any report to be written. It must impress. Like the blurb on a book's flyleaf or back cover, this short statement will sell your report. Don't leave writing the summary to the last ten minutes!

- Decide what is important. If you were forced to reduce your report to half a page, what would you most want to save? Write these essential points in a few sentences, stressing conclusions, recommendations and action points.

- Background: what does the reader need to know to understand the context of these few points? The summary must be able to stand on its own. Include too much rather than too little.

- Link these two sections into prose. Use paragraphs and layout to emphasize the most important points.

- Check and reduce. Cut out:

    repetition
    lists
    inessential detail
    unnecessary jargon
    examples
    numbers except where absolutely necessary (e.g. Recommendations)

The final version should be about half a page long. Ask a colleague to read it. Does it make sense as a separate item?

TITLE PAGE

Any but the shortest reports should put the title on a separate page, which will normally include:

- title: the biggest and boldest element

- author's name

- date

- reference number

- receiver's name or signature

- company name, address, or logo

- confidentiality mark

- copy number (for restricted reports)

Give thought to your title. It should be precise but brief. Balancing these two requirements can be tricky. A stylish solution is to give the report a main title followed by a longer, explanatory sub-title:

BIGGER AND BETTER
A strategy for growth in the next decade

LAYOUT

Layout displays the shape of your thoughts on the page. Above all, it should be **consistent** throughout the report.

- Display section numbers and page numbers clearly

- Number pages throughout

- Use a new page for each new section

- Indent sub-sections

- Emphasize headings and sub-headings — in a consistent style

- Use wide margins

- Double-spacing can be helpful

- Avoid right justification: it makes for a boring 'look'

- Use lists as much as possible.

ILLUSTRATIONS

A picture can be worth a thousand words — *if* it's the right picture!

A good illustration is relevant and useful. It should give one piece of information at a glance. If it's not essential to the argument, it shouldn't be used.

- Consider the best place for illustrations: main body or appendix?

- Keep them simple

- Refer to them in the text

- Introduce: present the picture; discuss it

- Call all illustrations 'Figures': each with a title and number

- Use fold-outs for illustrations referred to more than once

- Surround each Figure with lots of space on the page

- Prefer landscape to portrait format (horizontal edges longer than vertical)

- Beware copyright with material from other sources

CHECKING

Check each section as you finish it. It will save time later.

Try to leave as much time as possible between completing the first draft and checking it. Read the whole report in one go. Mark any passages obviously needing attention.

Is your report:

- *Clear?*

  – does it say what you want it to say? Is it persuasive?

- *Concise?*

  – is it all expressed as well as possible? Is there any repetition or padding?

- *Complete?*

  – is any information missing? Are any pages missing?

- *Correct?*

  – are facts and figures accurate? Do they support your conclusions? Are your recommendations realistic?

Next comes the painstaking task of detailed checking. It must be done; and done well. Never revise closely for more than 30 minutes at a time. Use a blank sheet of paper, moved down the page one line at a time, to help concentration.

Remember that reports can 'wander', either now or in the future. Your name is on the front page: your reputation may be on the line! Only by rigorous checking will you ensure that the final draft does you justice, and that all your hard work is handsomely reflected in the finished report.

3. MINUTES AND AGENDAS

Good minute-takers are worth their weight in gold. Yet too often the conditions to allow them to do their job well are not met: they are called in at a moment's notice and expected to take minutes without being made aware either of the purpose of the meeting, or of the names or functions of those present.

Minute-taking can only be effective as part of the process of organising the meeting. Along with the Chair, the Meeting Administrator is the most important person involved.

THE ROLE OF THE ADMINISTRATOR

As well as making all the physical arrangements for the meeting, the Administrator must notify all participants of the venue, date and time, send them copies of the agenda, and distribute any necessary papers. During the meeting, he or she will be on hand to deal with any problems, make sure that refreshments are available, and head off interruptions. After the meeting, any agreed actions must be followed up. All this, as well as taking, writing and distributing the minutes!

Obviously, the Administrator must be involved in all aspects of the meeting. Close liaison with the Chair is essential.

THE PRE-MEETING MEETING

It's a good idea, as preparation, to have a pre-meeting meeting between Chair and Administrator. It is an opportunity to clarify:

- **Why** the meeting is being held: its purpose; and why a meeting is necessary.

- **Who** will attend (and who will not); their function in the meeting, and the nature of their contributions; who is the Chair and who will take minutes.

- **When** the meeting will be held; when it will finish; how long each item will take; and times of breaks.

- **Where** the meeting will be held; where people will sit; whether any special equipment is required; and where the minute-taker will sit (where he or she can **see** everybody's face; **not** in the corner!).

- **What** the meeting will be about; what is the order of the items; what terminology will be used, and what it means; and what kind of minutes are needed.

Unless these questions are answered at this stage, the meeting is likely to be too long, confused, and unproductive.

It is critically important to establish the minute-taker's right to intervene during the meeting: to clarify procedure, decisions and agreed actions.

THE AGENDA

The immediate result of a pre-meeting meeting will be the agenda. It should be circulated about seven days in advance of the meeting. Sometimes a draft agenda is circulated for comments and then revised.

WHY HAVE AN AGENDA?

The word 'agenda' is Latin for 'things to be done'. It is a map of the journey the meeting will take. Its tasks are:

- to give advance warning to all participants;

- to state the purpose of the meeting;

- to indicate what preparation is required;

- to give the order of items;

- to give the Chair control of the meeting;

- to help the minute-taker to write up the minutes.

WHAT GOES ON THE AGENDA?

All agendas should include:

- the venue, date and time of the meeting;

- the name of the meeting, indicating its purpose;

- apologies for absence;

- the read and agreed minutes of the previous meeting;

- matters arising from those minutes;

- items in the main part of the meeting;

- the venue, date and time of the next meeting (including the all-important: 'Please bring your diary')

- the time the meeting will end.

The items during the body of the meeting should:

- have titles that are brief, specific and action-centred;

- be clear as to procedure (presentation; guest speaker; discussion of a report; a motion to be debated);

- include the names of contributors;

- be allocated a specific length of time.

Use a pattern plan to gather and organise the material that will be covered during the body of the meeting. The order of items can be crucial to the meeting's success. Put urgent but quick items first, longer items for discussion later. Give close attention to timing: no meeting, or part of a meeting, should last for more than 90 minutes without a break.

Avoid 'Any other business'. It is a pretext for old grudges to reappear and for old scores to be settled; too often it is used as an opportunity to hijack a meeting.

If something is worth discussing, it should be included as an item on the agenda. If the agenda is circulated in draft to all participants, there should be no excuse for complaint that an important matter is being ignored. In a real emergency, the Chair can amend the agenda at the beginning of the meeting.

MINUTES

What are minutes? The very word suggests something brief: a summary of events. Minutes are **not** a word-by-word description of all that is said in a meeting. The term 'verbatim minutes' is a contradiction in terms. A record of every word spoken requires a tape-recorder or stenographer: the result is a transcript, like *Hansard*.

Minutes are a record of discussion, decisions, and agreed actions. They should be accurate and objective; their style should be crisp and clear. Above all: they should be ***brief!***

WHY HAVE MINUTES?

Minutes perform a number of vital functions:

- a permanent record of what happened;

- evidence for legal or professional reasons;

- a reminder of actions to be done;

- an aid in writing the next agenda.

WHAT GOES ON THE MINUTES?

All minutes should follow the agenda exactly. They should include:

- the name of the meeting;
- the venue, date and time;
- names of participants;
- Apologies for absence;
- where necessary, 'Minutes read agreed and signed';
- where necessary, 'Matters arising';
- a record of the meeting, item by item, numbered exactly as on the agenda;
- a wide left margin, and a column of about a third of a page width on the right;
- actions noted and highlighted in the right-hand column, with names or initials and deadlines;
- the date of writing and at least one signature. Usually the minutes will be signed by minute-taker and chairperson.

MINUTE-TAKING SKILLS

Minute-taking involves three main skills:

LISTENING

— not just hearing what is said, but identifying the central points: the core of an argument, the crucial piece of information, the final decision, the agreed action.

Don't be seduced into trying to note everything that is said. Avoid shorthand for this reason.

If you have established your right to intervene during the meeting, your questions asking for clarification — where are we in the agenda? what decision has been reached? what is going to happen? who is responsible? — will help you to take accurate notes.

EDITING

You cannot listen and write at the same time. The trick is to find a way of note-taking that allows you to listen.

A *minute book,* hard–backed and A4 size, works like this:

1. Each item on the agenda has a separate page.
2. Each page is ruled into three columns: the central one is half the width of the page.
3. Column 1 for names of speakers;
   Column 2 for keywords of the discussion;
   Column 3 for actions and information.
4. Minutes in *note form.* Leave at least half a page space at the end of each item for late additions.
5. Actions in Column 3, perhaps using different colours to highlight. Include deadlines and names or initials of person responsible, and deadlines. *Information* is material to be passed on to people not at the meeting.

Pattern planning can be applied very successfully to minute-taking.

1. Use plain paper, at least A4 size. One sheet per item. Put the item number and name in a circle in the middle of the page. Blanks can be prepared before the meeting. Have pens of three colours available.
2. Work round the sheet clockwise, perhaps starting at '12 o'clock'. Note down key ideas as they arise, with initials if appropriate.
3. Use different colours for actions and information.

The great advantage of this method is that you can follow the course of the discussion, wherever it goes, and, at the same time, organise the material into a logical structure. It forces you to listen creatively, as there is only room for keywords, and encourages you to find the connections between ideas.

WRITING

Lengthy minutes will not be read. There is no virtue in painstaking descriptions of every parry and thrust: your readers want to know primarily what was decided and what will be done.

Write up the minutes as soon as possible after the meeting: within 24 hours if you can. Follow the 10-point plan for rewriting to check what you have written, paying particular attention to the following:

OBJECTIVITY

Of course minutes must be unbiased, but this does not mean that they must be expressed throughout in the passive voice:

Many opinions were voiced . . .
It was generally agreed . . .
It was thought necessary to . . .
The resolution was not passed . . .
The plans were considered at length . . .

Allocate responsibility by converting passive verbs to active ones:

Everybody expressed an opinion . . .
The committee agreed . . .
The Personnel Director thought it necessary to . . .
We could not pass the resolution . . .
The meeting considered the plans . . .

Remember, too, that minutes are not a record of everything that was said. Avoid the "He said, she said" syndrome! Unless a participant requests that a remark be noted in the minutes, concentrate on resolutions, decisions, and actions agreed.

TENSE

Generally, statements of what actually took place at the meeting should be in the past tense.

Tom presented a report on current car fleet usage.

Don't feel, however, that you must be rigorously consistent in your use of past tenses: the result will be 'minutespeak', which is unnatural and cumbersome:

Tom presented a report on current car fleet usage. He revealed that some sales staff were still claiming for unreasonably high mileage figures. After some discussion, it was agreed that Tom would continue to monitor expense forms and would report back to the committee at the next meeting.

As the minutes are dated, the present tense is quite acceptable for ongoing actions or opinions.

Some sales staff are still claiming for unreasonably high mileage figures.

Use the future for actions to be taken:

Tom will continue to monitor expense forms and report back at the next meeting.

The resulting minute is still accurate, far more brief and crystal clear.

There is no golden rule that minutes must be written in sentences. Abbreviated notes are often just as effective:

Tom's report: current car fleet usage. Continued unreasonable mileage claims from some sales staff. Tom to continue to monitor forms and report back.